LAW, MORALITY, AND WAR
IN THE
CONTEMPORARY WORLD

PRINCETON STUDIES IN WORLD POLITICS
Number 5

PRINCETON STUDIES IN WORLD POLITICS

Law, Morality, and War
in the
Contemporary World

RICHARD A. FALK

Published for the Center of International Studies
Princeton University

FREDERICK A. PRAEGER, *Publisher*
New York · London

Frederick A. Praeger, Publisher
64 University Place, New York 3, N.Y., U.S.A.
49 Great Ormond Street, London W.C. 1, England

Published in the United States of America in 1963 by
Frederick A. Praeger, Inc., Publisher

Library of Congress Catalog Card Number: 63-13680

Printed in the United States of America

Preface

What precautions can be taken to avoid the outbreak of nuclear war without clearing obstacles from the path of the aggressor? This book attempts an answer from the perspective of law and morality. The avoidance of nuclear war realistically requires basic structural changes in world affairs. A warless world presupposes the elimination of large national defense establishments, a non-nuclearly equipped international police force, and some form of world government that is endowed with limited legislative competence. It is essential to terminate national control over the use of force in international relations. Such an objective constitutes a practical policy; it is no longer a fanciful program for dreamers. Nevertheless, the prospect for realizing a new world order under central institutions remains rather dim. The need has yet to foster the will.

We find instead that the settled habits and prerogatives of nations are slow to give way, especially in periods of crisis and fear. Thus it is not surprising that we have an arms race of unprecedented magnitude rather than a serious effort to change the international system sufficiently to institutionalize the maintenance of peace. Reluctantly, one concludes that possession and proliferation of nuclear weapons exercise less influence upon the orientation of national behavior and outlook than do traditional pursuits of power, wealth, and prestige. It is true that nations seem generally aware that their survival depends more upon stable patterns of mutual restraint than upon the capacity to win a major war. This generates a new contemporary ratio between risk and national policy that gives strong emphasis to the virtues of military prudence. It does not, however, induce the perception that the protection of national interests involves the destruction of the military capacity to wage thermonuclear war. These comments apply mainly to the bilateral context of Soviet-American relations, although alliance networks, collective defense arrangements, bloc politics, and global fallout disclose a universal involvement in the hazards that attend the development of weaponry.

We operate, then, with a dual awareness: first, a sense of futility about the possibilities for basic transformations of the international system in the years ahead; second, a widespread and inhibiting recognition of the destructive potential of nuclear warfare. This shifts realistic emphasis to an examination of what can be done to make the outbreak of nuclear war less probable if we assume a reasonably constant context for international politics. Such an endeavor bears directly upon the selection of a defense strategy, the improvement of command and control arrangements, the nontransfer of nuclear weapons, the elimination of military adventuring and rash politics, a reasonably conciliatory approach to crisis and conflict, the transmission of information that gives a potential enemy reassurance about the renunciation of offensive uses of international force, and various constraints upon military research and development to avoid the creation of yet more unstable military instruments (e.g., chemical, radiological, biological, and fusion weapons).

This essay tries to complement these inquiries by describing some of the contributions that can be made by law and morality to an international regime of restraint that is designed to minimize the risks of nuclear war without increasing the vulnerability of nations to direct or indirect aggression. The novelty of the age has made law and morality appear obsolete for the conduct of international affairs. The pressure of the times has led nations to grow insensitive to restraining norms. This results in the neglect of our two strongest cultural traditions of restraint. It is hoped that this essay will demonstrate the relevance of law and morality to the common goal of the avoidance of major war. Our normative heritage is a resource that we can no longer afford to squander.

In the course of writing several drafts of this essay I have received valuable encouragement and criticism from many people. This made me continue work on a subject that often seemed to transcend my competence and elude my understanding. I feel, therefore, especially beholden to friends and critics; in this case a formal acknowledgment is even more than usual a rather feeble gesture to adumbrate a profound sense of gratitude.

The research and writing were done under the beneficial auspices of the Center of International Studies. I am particularly grateful to Klaus Knorr, the Director of the Center, for doing so much to create a scholarly atmosphere, as well as for making many detailed and perceptive suggestions that led me to a deeper awareness of my own subject. His friendship and encouragement, despite some disagreements with my basic outlook, give rise to special feelings of appreciation.

My serious concern with the interrelation of force, law, and morality in world affairs commenced in response to an invitation to write an article for the *Natural Law Forum*. The Editor of this important journal, John T. Noonan, Jr., made a series of illuminating comments that led me to expand considerably the scope of inquiry.

Myres S. McDougal has shaped my view of international law as a teacher, author, and friend. My debts to him are so obvious that acknowledgment is unnecessary and yet so fundamental that acknowledgment is an outrageous understatement. Professor McDougal has saved me from several oversights by his careful reading of the manuscript.

In addition, I am most indebted to Erich Kahler for sharing with me, in a series of conversations, often heated but always rewarding, his profound interpretation of the impact of nuclear weapons upon human destiny. My gratitude is also owed to Morton A. Kaplan for his most constructive criticism of two versions of this manuscript. In addition, I wish to thank John B. Putnam for his valuable editorial assistance. Peter Paret, Thornton Read, Sidney Verba, Andrew Janos, Davis Bobrow, James Rosenau, Philip Green, and Earl Finbar Murphy each contributed criticisms that have changed the final product. Sally Appleton, Norman Indictor, and Alan S. Oser have spared me some stylistic misjudgments.

Finally, it is a pleasure to acknowledge the cheerful indulgence of the Center's stenographic staff. In particular, I wish to thank Jean McDowall for her thoughtful management of my successive drafts and Judy Sims and Constance Ducey for the actual typing.

Such a long list of acknowledgments for such a short book makes me fully aware of the happy extent to which authorship can become a collaborative enterprise. Of course, my dependence on the scholarly spirit of community cannot spare me full responsibility for whatever remains arch, wrong, or imprecise in the pages that follow. As it is, the subject that I write upon is so littered with controversy that tolerance, more than assent, is my primary wish. The diverse responses to the crisis brought on by the military development of nuclear energy are a powerful testimony to the health of our free society.

RICHARD A. FALK

Woods Hole, Mass.
June 21, 1962

Contents

Contents

I

A Partial Framework for
Moral Judgment

> Our foremost aim is the control of force, not the
> pursuit of force, in a world made safe for man-
> kind.
> —PRESIDENT JOHN F. KENNEDY[1]

> I believe the present international system to be
> one which has a significant probability built into
> it of irretrievable disaster for the human race.
> —KENNETH E. BOULDING[2]

One of man's most profound quests is for knowledge about
the proper use and control of force in human relations. Force
entails a vital range of claims over life and death. Thus it becomes imperative to use force as beneficially as possible. This
requires a delicate balance between use and control. In
world affairs, nuclear technology creates an imbalance that
threatens us with catastrophe. In such a situation it is essential to strengthen all means of control that are at our disposal.
This essay contends that law and morality offer potentialities
for control that have not yet been adequately appreciated.

The legal order is given major responsibility for the management of force in domestic society. The progress of centuries has tended to make the legal management of domestic
force more rational and humane. Despite this progress, difficult and unsolved problems continue to exacerbate civilized
societies. Consider, for instance, the current American debates about capital punishment or the use of lethal weapons

to keep neighbors and friends out of fallout shelters; or arguments for and against the Negro sit-in movement in the South that often center upon the moral bases for the use of private coercion that is alleged to violate the positive law. The celebrated dialogue between Camus and Sartre on terrorism in Algeria vividly depicts the search for authoritative limits upon the role of domestic force.

Yet how much more difficult is it to define the proper use of international force.[3] For the absence of unified institutional control, the diversity of cultural attitudes, the conflict of political and ideological rivals, and the enormity of the destructive potential confront mankind with a variety of tragic prospects. Most immediately we think of nuclear devastation and totalitarian domination. But this quick discernment is also quick deception: To discern truly, we must face the *unequal* and *uncertain* risks of various kinds of warfare and the *imponderable* risks of different forms of totalitarian encroachment. It is the rational selection of risks, not the contemplation of extreme failures of policy, that must engage our creative moral energies.[5] Too often, however, the jurist evades this framework of inquiry, focusing instead on the sufficiency or insufficiency of existing legal rules to achieve the control of aggressive force.[6] The relevance of the political environment to the role and function of law is neglected. And yet the nuclear arms race goes on, and crisis situations (especially in Europe) are frequently seen as leading directly to at least limited nuclear warfare if a breakdown of the present fragile *modus vivendi* takes place.

Carl Mayer depicts this uneasy state of world politics by saying: "The *pax atomica* is a *pax timoris*, based on a balance of terror with all that this implies." Mayer adds that "the peace of the world" is necessarily fragile, most often resembling "an armed truce" rather than a condition of international harmony.[7] The *pax atomica* is an instance, then, of the normal quality of peaceful relations. Its apparent uniqueness disappears when one assumes a historical perspective. Mayer suggests sin as the explanation for the persistent inability of man to achieve a condition of peace that is based on harmony of interests rather than on mutual fear. An emphasis upon sin connects the problem of war with the fundamental state of human nature. It suggests the difficulty of overcoming the high order of threats posed by the development of nuclear weapons and guidance systems. Nothing less than a basic change in human nature is required. The achievement of a warless world involves much more than the design of a formal arrangement for the use and control of force.

Mayer's religious statement of the root difficulty (sin) is a jolting reminder that proposing to end warfare may be like mounting wax wings to fly beneath the sun. For if war is a product of sin and sin is a legacy of the forbidden fruit taken from the tree of knowledge, then a state of enduring peace requires a symbolic or material return to the unique harmonies of the Garden of Eden. Regardless of whether one accepts this religious style of explanation, it expresses realistically the magnitude of the task and the naïveté of all those who think that the burden of warfare can be overcome by proposals, however rational. We find, lurking beneath a contemporary exterior of despair, what amounts to a subversive variety of optimism on the part of all those who conceive transition to a warless world in purely intellectual terms—finding a plan and putting it into existence. Candor demands that men acknowledge their apparent helplessness to establish the conditions for permanent peace on earth. Such an acknowledgment does not intend to interfere with the quest but merely predicts a dire outcome if one is willing to take experience and reality seriously.

This portrayal of human nature does not imply the futility of law or morality. Man's hostile disposition may preclude the establishment of permanent peace, but it does not suggest that human behavior is unresponsive to restraining claims. In fact, the relevance of law and morality to human affairs rests firmly upon the premise of imperfection. Otherwise, restraint would be an unnecessary inhibition upon human freedom. This background prompts the present essay on the bearing of the intertwining perspectives of law, morality, and social policy upon the contemporary use of international force. It inclines more toward the discovery of guidelines, problems, and dilemmas than toward the proposal of solutions. It is discomforting to discover that evident solutions either blunt the cutting edge of social reality or muffle the claims of social conscience. The utopian dreamer and the mere military pragmatist are each guilty of grave error in their response to the world. We must suppress our longing for immediate and final solutions; genuine moral encounter requires that we choose only from among those genuine possibilities implicit within the living tissue of human affairs. This forbearance at the present stage of history imposes a life of incredible danger and tension once we grow aware of its terrifying dimensions.

An inquiry into the morality of war is beset by doubts of a most fundamental quality. Can we ever justify the use of lethal force by man against man? Do we not minimize the inherent immorality of war by explicating the conditions that vindicate the use of national coercion? Ronald Steel updates the basic dilemma as follows: "The lot of the war moralist has never been an easy one. To reconcile unattainable goals with unjustifiable means is surely the most thankless of tasks. And to attempt this labor in the context of nuclear war is simply to invite disbelief."[8]

But there is the other side of the dilemma that insists upon moral discourse. Mankind depends everywhere upon the use of lethal force to regulate and protect the common good against external compulsion. The alternative to war is to give way to the violator of the peace, no matter how evil. The basis for inquiry, then, is established by the acceptance of force as a necessary incident of intrasocietal and intersocietal conflict. Law and morality seek to assure the beneficial management of force, to restrain its deployment by the acceptance of limitations upon its use and the intensity of its application. Especially in an era of nuclear technology it is essential to clarify the standards that govern the use of force in human affairs.

All dominant social orders accept as routine certain uses for lethal force. If a man approaches with a gun and threatens my life, I or a spectator may prevent this by killing him, if necessary. Police protection extends to international killing. Similarly, the protection of a national community from external armed attack gives rise to an unquestioned right to resist. That is, prevailing cultural values almost everywhere authorize recourse to lethal force under appropriate circumstances of danger and attack. The ubiquity of authorization is not a demonstration of the moral correctness of defensive force, but it is a suitable starting point for a discussion of ethical principles. We are less interested in discerning ultimate moral foundations for conduct than in specifying the moral restraints that apply to conduct authorized, in general, by prevailing values.

The subject of international force presents crucial issues of choice upon a terrain where our social commitments appear to be morally problematic, intellectually confused, and politically weak. The advent of nuclear weapons gives dramatic urgency to an inquiry into the moral bases for the use of force in international affairs.[9] The macabre prospect of nuclear devastation tends to paralyze moral sensibilities, often producing amoral responses such as indifference and bewilderment. This situation produces a moral vacuum. However, the political conflicts and challenges of the time compel responsible leaders to make choices and adopt policies. The consequence is that decision-making contexts are unable to assimilate moral considerations. In the light of this situation, it is hardly surprising that the most influential writing about the use of nuclear weapons tends either to ignore the moral dimension or to be unsophisticated about the complexities of military planning.[10]

idea

Legal norms generated by the international system provide an appropriate basis for reflection and evaluation. Two distinct objectives are sought. First, this essay examines some of the special problems created by existing legal norms governing the use of force in the international society of today. These problems become more evident when we consider that nuclear weapons, totalitarianism, colonial domination, and the Cold War are present in a modern world composed of more than a hundred nations, each claiming "sovereignty" for itself. Second, we propose to explore existing and plausible patterns of justification that govern the use of international force. This requires us to distinguish force of varying intensities as used in a series of specific situations.

It would appear that the high costs and the risks of force in international affairs presuppose that a responsible decision to use force would include a serious attempt to find an adequate prior justification that engages in an exhaustive search for alternatives, even risky alternatives (or substitutes). "Justification" refers to the range of considerations more usually identified as "the moral dimension" or "human conscience." "Justification" is a referent that expresses a moral context without requiring us to enter the debate between the various types of natural law and the several versions of legal positivism.[11] In this essay I am not directly concerned with the ontal status or truth claims that can be or are made on behalf of a particular pattern of justification.

Even in such a foreshortened range of moral inquiry, however, it is necessary to make clear the framework within which it operates. This framework consists largely of certain moral and political predispositions toward the use of force in international affairs today. These predispositions rest upon the acceptance of a line of interpretation and argument. It will clarify the analysis that follows if the major elements of the moral framework used are suggested in summary form. However, it is important to distinguish these moral presuppositions from other kinds of rules that govern national behavior in the world today. There is no necessary coincidence of moral and legal norms, although adherence to law rests ultimately upon the moral confirmation of its rules. The moral refusal to allow a nation to initiate the use of nuclear weapons is coupled, it will be seen, with the discernment of a legal tolerance for their initial use if essential for territorial self-defense after an armed attack has taken place.[12]

1. A Rejection of Military Autonomy

Prudential judgments about the uses of international force are unacceptable if they seek only to maximize military goals that are at stake.[13] A sufficient justification for uses of international force always carries the decision-maker beyond the battlefield to examine the relevance of law, morality, and politics. We must restrict this observation to general authorizations of the use of force, not specific tactical decisions within an existing arena of violent conflict.

It may seem unnecessary to dwell upon an insistence that appears so obvious from the perspective of detached observation. But, in fact, there is a tendency under the pressure of circumstance to accept a military commitment, once it is made explicit, as an absolute obligation that cannot later be withdrawn for moral or political reasons. For instance, the defense of West Berlin often appears to operate as a fixed coordinate in Western thinking. We reject such rigidity whenever it entails the use of substantial quantities of force or appears dangerously provocative of general war. Instead, it is urged that there exists a continuous need to rejustify decisions entailing substantial force in the light of values other than a particular military victory or defeat. The controversy about whether to carry the Korean War beyond the Yalu, although stable in military rhetoric, was primarily a conflict between a policy that absolutized military objectives and a policy that sought to moderate the military context by guarding against escalation.[14] Adherence to the rule restricting the use of force to Korean territory provided both belligerents with a mutual standard of limitation. If the objective of winning the Korean War (rather than tolerating a stalemate) was accorded paramountcy, then the stability of the limiting standard would have been lost. Such reasoning works reciprocally, accounting, we suppose, for the failure of North Korean forces to bomb supply depots in Japan.

Restraint in warfare should not merely reflect the outer limit of what it is militarily advantageous to do in order to bring victory in a conflict. Most definitely, the decision to use nuclear weapons must be confirmed by considerations of non-military necessity deriving from acceptable moral and political commitments. The military calculus is just one aspect of the complex endeavor to justify uses of force in international affairs.

Frequently, we hear it said that United States participation in the anti-Castro invasion of Cuba in April, 1961, was reprehensible primarily because of the failure to use sufficient force to achieve the objectives of the intervention. This position does highlight the apparent immorality of sponsoring a military adventure that brings death and destruction to many of the participants and yet contains little hope for a successful outcome. This amounts to a sacrificial use of force that is perhaps justifiable as symbolic resistance or martyrdom but is not normally acceptable. The surrender of objectives rather than their hopeless pursuit by lethal means is itself an attribute of political morality.

However, if the criticism of the insufficiency of the Cuban invasion is oblivious to the moral significance of attempts to economize the use of international force—its quantum, intensity, scope, and duration—or disregards possible adverse effects—as for instance, an analogous imposition of Soviet will upon Finland—then the advocacy of sufficient force is itself immoral according to the standards urged in this essay. Political objectives justify a certain level of force and no more. It is one thing to contemplate nuclear retaliation for the defense of the United States after a prior nuclear attack; it is another to undertake a nuclear defense of Quemoy and Matsu (as 55 per cent of Americans were reported willing to do).[15] It is part of our thesis that the morality of international force requires nations to take every precaution to minimize the use of force in world affairs.

The Cuban invasion illustrates also the tendency of evaluation to detach itself from restraining norms of law and morality. Before we can justify a quantum of force sufficient to attain a political objective—say, the overthrow of Castro by a liberal democratic elite—it is essential to justify the recourse to force itself. Sponsorship of the Cuban invasion apparently required the United States to violate clear legal rules contained in a series of applicable treaties and to join with rebel exiles to use force against the internal claims of sovereignty made by the legitimate (Castro) Cuban Government.[16] It is hence difficult to criticize only the *failure* of the invasion and not the invasion itself if we accept the restraints imposed by law and morality upon *national* discretion to use force across boundaries.[17] Yet many appraise such an event by exclusive reference to its success or failure. Morton A. Kaplan, a most acute analyst of world affairs, expressed this form of response: "Intervention as such [in Cuba] was undoubtedly a sound policy, for the present world is not a world in which non-intervention is possible. It is, however, the effectiveness of policy that is important and it was with respect to effectiveness that American policy in Cuba failed."[18] Behind this comment lies the insight that interdependence makes adherence to norms of nonintervention impossible and that, therefore, nations should use their power to the extent necessary—"It is the . . . effectiveness of policy that is important"—for the achievement of national goals. Such a prescription, if not significantly qualified, overlooks the dangers of unrestraint in world affairs. Intervention may be inevitable, but the use of certain coercive instruments, the principal source of danger, is avoidable. Norms of morality and law seek control over behavior that threatens to undermine minimum stability. Respect for these norms is critical in a world where nations judge the worth of their own goals from contradictory ethical perspectives and possess weapons that threaten mutual destruction.

Stable patterns of restraint depend upon the consistent relevance of restraining norms of law and morality, not just their expedient relevance. Claims of military necessity should not be allowed to overwhelm our moral and legal sensibilities, especially in a world where national security increasingly becomes a function of mutual restraint rather than the achievement of decisive weapons superiority.

2. A Rejection of Preventive War and Pre-emptive Strategies

It is not justifiable for one nation to initiate an armed attack across an international boundary regardless of provocation. Of course, it is difficult to specify the quality of an armed attack so as to distinguish it from lesser uses of force such as border raids or guerrilla penetrations. The emphasis here is upon a sustained use of military force by nations against one another to achieve fundamental alterations in the nation that is the target of attack.[19] The reference is to intersocietal violence, thus distinguishing all participations that result from intervention in an intra-societal conflict. Particular reference is made here to the use of international force to forestall or frustrate an anticipated attack by the enemy. Such a concern accepts as a moral premise the status of war as a provisional evil, justifiable only if fought as a defense against a prior armed attack. This premise carries forward the normative commitment of the Charter of the United Nations, which obliges members to renounce national uses of force across boundaries except for purposes of individual or collective self-defense within the terms of Article 51.[20]

The need for a firm norm prohibiting an initial use of force is made imperative by the character of the nuclear threat. The fear of surprise attack and the rapidity of missile delivery by the other side induces anticipatory force to protect national capacities for defense, especially if the enemy's first-strike delivery system is vulnerable and the pre-emptive state's counterstrike capacity is vulnerable. The possible magnitude of a single nuclear attack gives particular emphasis to rules and conditions that prevent its commencement. It is desirable to implement the rule by making second-strike capacities invulnerable, thereby undercutting the temptation to hit first either to immobilize the enemy or to pre-empt a supposed attack.[21] This is an important area of concern, since the fear of surprise attack, the advantages of a first strike, the possibilities of "incontrovertible intelligence" reports of an enemy plan to attack, the vulnerability of a counterstrike capacity, and the speed of missile delivery systems constitute rational bases for recourse to pre-emptive or preventive strategies. It is imperative to guard against hazards of judgments provoked by crisis and fear. One form of protection is the acceptance of fixed standards of limitation, asserting the primacy of directive principles over contextual judgments. An initiating use of force, even nuclear force, may proceed upon as firm a ground of justification as a decision to employ defensive force, but the peculiar danger of conferring this discretion supports its prohibition. As a matter of principle, we guard against fallibility and misplaced zeal by eliminating discretion to initiate the use of international force. The principle, hence, operates as a substitute for judgment, imposing inflexibility in exchange for the lessening dangers of flexibility.

Of course, the acceptance of this renunciation of force seems to interfere with the deterrence of provocative conduct. An aggressor nation, aware of the renunciation of prior recourse to force as a matter of effective principle, is assured that it will not meet military opposition unless it carries out its expansionist policy by means of an armed attack across a recognized international frontier. Avenues of so-called indirect aggression (subversion and intervention) seem broad enough to accommodate the expansionist pressures of modern states. especially if the alternative is nuclear warfare. The prudential response of nations concerned with containment is to discover adequate defensive measures that do not depend upon international (border-crossing) force.[22] In addition to the failure of "massive retaliation" to create a credible policy for discouraging provocative action short of an armed attack, it departs from the central moral directive to place proportional limitations upon the use of counterforce, no matter how defensive; as well, it appears to violate Article 51 of the United Nations Charter. The main consideration here is that the vulnerability of *status quo* nations to indirect aggression is not accepted as a moral justification that warrants recourse to international force. Instead, alternative strategies of defense that limit that arena of violent conflict to a single nation are treated as mandatory.

There are two positions taken here. First, no provocative action other than an armed attack (within the meaning of Article 51) across an international frontier warrants the use of military force by one nation against another. Although this assertion seems clear enough, specifying conditions for its fulfillment are not. For instance, unclear boundaries, such as exist in Southeast Asia, make it exceedingly difficult to identify boundary-crossing. If two nations each claim the same area as "national territory," then there is no automatic distinction between internal and international uses of force. Second, under no circumstances except in the event of a nuclear armed attack is it permissible to have recourse to nuclear weapons; a state must defend itself with conventional arms against a non-nuclear armed attack even if the alternative to the initiation of nuclear war is national surrender.[23] In effect, this prohibition limits the pretensions of sovereign discretion over national defense to military means short of initial recourse to nuclear weapons. An analogous prohibition, preformed by legal prescription, claims control over the use of poisonous gas. The permissive exception exists in the form of reprisal, not defensive necessity.[24] This withdraws the decision to use from subjective factors (the appraisal of need) and makes an objective event critical (an actual use violating the moral principle and derivative norm). Such an objective regime makes patterns of behavior more stable, less prone to extreme responses under the pressure of an emergency. These attempts to contain deteriorations of peaceful relations are an essential aspect of the struggle to stabilize international relations.[25]

It should be observed that this restraining norm based upon moral considerations is unlikely to elicit respect in the event that a nation must choose between an advantageous initiation of nuclear weapons and a serious military defeat. Western leaders, reacting to Sino-Soviet geopolitical and manpower advantages, seem reluctant to renounce the option to initiate nuclear war in the face of severe Soviet provocation.

This attitude discloses a characteristic refusal of nations to circumscribe the flexibility of their recourse to self-defense.[26] By allowing nuclear weapons to be used in self-defense as a matter of law, there is made an effort to reconcile legal norms with political reality. At the same time, an insistence upon a contradictory moral norm calls into question the prevailing patterns of military posture.

3. The Limit of Self-Defense

There is often a contrast between national reluctance to initiate war and the unrestraint that accompanies defensive uses of force by a nation responding to an armed attack against it.[27] This contrast is especially prevalent in United States thinking and behavior, reflecting perhaps a lack of experience with uses of force in the balance-of-power period of European history when the pursuit of limited political objectives even in time of war was a dominant political norm. An insistence upon "unconditional surrender" is a characteristic attitude of the mentality of absolute defense. At minimum, uses of force must be pursued to a point where it can be said that "victory" results. General MacArthur sought to

conduct the Korean War on this basis. Restraint was imposed
in Korea by our civilian leadership for prudential reasons—
to avoid escalation and to stop an unpopular and misunder-
stood war.

Why should the right of self-defense carry with it an authorization for the pursuit of political objectives that would
be otherwise illegitimate? For example, the right of self-determination is suddenly made subject to the dispositions of
the defending nation, but only if it has the strength and the
will to prevail in a total sense. It is possible to argue that this
form of unrestricted response deters aggressive uses of force.
A nation will hesitate less to use force if it can rely upon the
limited character of the defensive response. In addition, one
can argue rather convincingly that an aggressive use of force
renders the attacking nation subject to the will of the international community. That is, the concept of nonintervention
and neutrality insulates a nation only so long as it does not
make an armed attack across an international frontier. However, if it attacks, then the defending nation and its friends
are entitled to make any response that fulfills their preferences and expresses their capabilities. The use of atomic
bombs at Hiroshima and Nagasaki dramatically illustrates
this logic and its supporting ethic. The refusal to moderate
Allied war objectives, the unwillingness to make a demonstration bombing in an uninhabited area, and the callous disregard of suffering that authorized the Nagasaki bomb illustrate an extreme form of tolerance for the claims of defensive
force.

It may clarify the moral and legal status of this claim if we
examine it from the perspective of a domestic social order.
In domestic society we accept readily the authority of the
community to impose its will whenever someone resorts to
unauthorized lethal violence. The pursuit of criminal be-

havior acts to forfeit at least part of the claim of an individual
to life, liberty, and the pursuit of happiness. Does not an
aggressor nation stand in the same relation to international
society than an individual bears to domestic society? The analogy does help to illuminate the problem. In advanced domestic societies an individual is usually able to pursue just
grievances without recourse to force. Furthermore, the domestic victim of an armed attack is not entitled to do more
than protect himself, using the minimum force needed to
achieve this end. Any further sanction is a matter for legal
prosecution, conviction, and judgment. There is a general
effort to make the sanction proportionate to the seriousness
of the offense. Even when the victim of an attack dies from
it, there is disagreement about whether the social order is entitled to impose a capital sanction. If the victim survives, then
the law moderates its response. Not since the harsh times of
Jean Valjean has society necessarily sought to impose death or
unlimited sanctions upon a criminal defendant.

There are several points of reference to the situation in international relations. First, techniques of peaceful change
and protection against provocative harassment are often unavailable in the affairs of nation-states. This may make the
initiation of unauthorized violence a more ambiguous defi-
ance of the legal order and, hence, less deserving of a harsh
sanction. Second, the international system lacks regularly
available and impartial institutions to find facts and assess
legal responsibility. This means that greater reliance must be
placed upon the biased response of the victim. Although this
reliance is unavoidable in the first instance, it should at least
be moderated by fixed limitations that seek results somewhat
equivalent to the graduated scale of sanctions in domestic
society. Third, domestic societies do not claim absolute discretion over the destiny of someone who resorts to violence—

even lethal violence. However, a theory of unlimited defensive objectives makes every attacking state potentially subject to the absolute discretion of the victim, supplemented perhaps by the participation of other nations and possibly supported by the judgment and cooperation of international organizations.

Without attempting a detailed position, this essay proposes to limit defensive force *as employed by nations* to the approximate restoration of the *status quo ante*. The coercive pursuit of additional objectives by the defensive nation(s) requires, at least, the formal authorization of an appropriate organ of the United Nations. In this process, formal authorization and actual participation by regional institutions on the side of the defending nation should be given great weight.

The prudential basis for this norm is to impose a fairly definite limit upon the use of force by all participants in international armed conflict, regardless of where responsibility lies for the initiation of violence. This seems to be an essential brake upon escalation pressures. And it also acknowledges that although the distinction between "aggressor" and "defender" may serve usefully as a first approximation of national responsibility for the purpose of restoring *order*, it is insufficient to act as a guide to the ends of justice. An international organization should probably act to restore order on behalf of the defender nation, but the task of designing an optimum disposition of the conflict is a matter for polycentric community judgment.

The traditional techniques used to restrain the scope and intensity of warfare have been rendered almost meaningless in the context of nuclear warfare. The level of anticipated destruction is so high that distinctions between military and nonmilitary targets, between combatants and civilians, between neutrals and belligerents, although still relevant, must

be understood in a vastly different sense. This makes it especially important to develop new techniques of limitation. The
confinement of defensive force to the recovery of the territorial *status quo* is recommended in response to the post-nu-
clear development of military technology. It satisfies some of
the need for moral and legal rules that reflect the extent to
which force grows unusable when it threatens to inflict intolerable levels of damage and suffering.

4. A Rejection of Nuclear Pacifism and Unilateral Disarmament

We consider here only radical refusals to reply upon the defense system to protect the security of the nation in a nuclear
age.[28] Such refusals should not be confused with an attitude
of unilateral initiative with regard to provocation, crisis, risk,
conflict, and tension. Drawing back from the brink is an attitude toward international affairs that is critically different
from an abandonment of a primary reliance upon a system of
nuclear deterrence.

Whereas pre-emptive strategies use force as a protective or
beneficial measures of political initiative, unilateralist strategies urge renunciations of nuclear force as the prime policy of
political initiative. There are many variants of the position
taken by the nuclear pacificist–unilateral disarmament
groups—[29] but the essential claim is that a reliance upon nuclear weapons for military defense is either wrong or impru-
dent, or both,[30] as the world presently exists. Several intersect-
ing lines of reasoning have been advanced to support this
radical optioning-out of the nuclear arms race. First, the pacificist ethic, especially after the successes of Gandhi and Martin
Luther King, appears to provide an effective alternative to the
use of lethal force to achieve political objectives; that is, force
is held to be either an autonomous wrong to be rejected re-

gardless of its efficacy, or it is a prudential wrong to be rejected because there exist less costly ways of attaining the goals that men seek. This argument often inverts the putative Marxist maxim that "The end justifies the means" to claim instead that the purity of the end depends upon the purity of the means. Such fundamental pacifism, at least as applied to world politics, has been defended by its adherents either because it is morally superior or because it is less risky and costly than reliance upon military defense. The prudential variation may also be limited to nuclear weapons, accepting conventional warfare as a permissible use of force.

Second, unilateral nuclear disarmament is urged as a decisive way to break the deadlock that seems to paralyze disarmament negotiations. Disarmament agreements between Cold War rivals appear difficult to achieve. Even if we presuppose mutual good faith, it is evident that nations are bargaining to acquire relative strategic advantages or to be sure to avoid strategic disadvantages in the disarming world as well as to achieve disarmament itself. This means that each side perceives the other as agreeing to a disarmament scheme only if its relative military position is thereby improved; thus military force may seem more, not less, usable in the early stages of disarmament as it may offer more prospects of successful deployments. This category of risk is intensified by the difficulty of finding formulas for equivalent reductions in military strength and the truly enormous problem of projecting these equivalences through time as technology, patterns of conflict, and defense strategies develop along asymmetrical lines. Thus, for instance, an inspection arrangement designed to detect nonatmospheric nuclear tests presently gives the United States the additional advantage of valuable information about the location of Soviet delivery systems without giving comparable advantages to the Soviet Union.[31]

A radical break-through, by way of comprehensive and general disarmament, achieved at a single stroke, is blocked by mutual distrust and by a variety of economic and political obstacles in all domestic societies, although most evidently in the West where major decisions presuppose legislative support and popular backing. The unilateralist response provides a way of moving into disarmament without the need for interim bargaining toward equivalences. Such unilateralism arises from a conviction that rival nations are or may be sincere about their commitment to disarmament but unable to fulfill it within the traditional framework of diplomatic negotiation. Unilateral initiative, it is urged, would undercut the psychological support for the arms race and tend to generate an atmosphere more conducive to the peaceful settlement of the East-West conflict.

Third, unilateralists point to the urgency of the existing situation claiming the need to work now for a break-through. Problems of Nth-Country, Nth-Crew, accidental, catalytic, and escalatory war contribute instability to a nuclear peace that rests upon deterrence and rationality. In such a situation, patient waiting for a solution *deus ex machina* is a vice. There is also the prevalent assumption, based on a partial reading of history, that arms buildups necessarily or, at least, most probably end in war. This anticipation is accompanied by the further assumption that nuclear war means a total war in which each side makes use of its entire nuclear capacity and thereby causes widespread annihilation of cities and populations. These dire prospects seem so much worse than any political outcome, however negative, that it leads adherents to prefer the risks or even the assurance of political defeat to the risks of nuclear warfare. This is the psychological basis for movements summarized by such slogans as "Better red than dead."

In opposition to the unilateralist position, however admirable and humane the motives of many of its advocates may be, there are several considerations that together lead to its rejection. First, it does not seem likely to generate enough popular support to become a viable political alternative for the United States.[32] In fact, unilateralist agitation of any real magnitude in the United States might well give political dominance to rightist groups and lead to a hardening of American foreign policy. Unilateralism can be expected to produce militarism rather than pacifism insofar as it succeeds at all as a mass movement. Such an ironic expectation is a somber complication for anyone who is seriously striving for peace and yet despairs of existing approaches. The alternatives to nuclear deterrence may be even more dangerous, despite elements of theoretical, ethical, and psychological attractiveness.[33] A major position of this essay is that the moralist must always undertake to envision the practical consequences of human action. It is part of the responsibility of relating human action to the distribution of power and values within the relevant social order. For only by knowing the values of those with significant access to power can we discern the limits of feasible advocacy.[34]

This calculation is reinforced by an assessment of Communist behavior in the Cold War. There is every indication of Soviet willingness to press political advantages whenever this can be done without serious risk of nuclear war. There is little evidence that the Soviet bloc is willing to settle for the political *status quo*.[35] Therefore, the only effective check upon Sino-Soviet expansion or attempts at nuclear blackmail is the presence of sufficient countervailing force to make the costs of conflict too high. Thus any unilateral reduction of Western military capacity merely invites proportionate Communist expansion. This is itself undesirable. Perhaps even more serious, however, is the tendency of Communist success to induce

rightist and militaristic reactions in the West. If Western political power further declines, the prospects of preventive and
suicidal wars of "defense" grow more probable. Hence anticipation of Communist response makes the unilateral program
more likely to increase, rather than to decrease, the likelihood
of general nuclear war, and for this reason its advocacy becomes ironically related to its goals.

Why should not the West accept current Soviet disarmament proposals rather than disarm unilaterally?[36] The statement of the question in this form uncovers the utopian
(detached from the realities of power) quality of the unilateralist position. Who would expect the United States
Senate by a two-thirds majority to ratify an American acceptance of the Soviet proposal? But if we cannot look toward
support in the United States for an official policy that involves
participation by the Soviet Union on its own terms, in a disarmament process, it is even less likely that such support will
develop for a course of action that leaves the Soviet bloc free
to follow an optimum military policy while the United States
and its allies gradually weaken their nuclear defense system.

We must remember that beneath the shared commitment
to nuclear peace persists a severe ideological and political
competition for power that would not necessarily diminish
because the threat of nuclear attack was reduced. In fact, the
elimination of the danger of nuclear war might be expected
to stimulate an intensification of the conflict with an en-
hanced role for force in world affairs.[37]

The unilateralists also appear to exaggerate the danger of
the existing defense system, as compared with alternatives.
There is considerable evidence of great care on the part of
nuclear antagonists on those occasions when overt conflicts, as
in Berlin, Cuba, or Hungary, lead national leaders to climb
higher on the escalation ladder. There seems to be an increas-

ing awareness that a nuclear war, whatever its outcome in the traditional terms of victory and defeat, would amount to a severe setback for every participant. Leaders of all nations seem united in their resolution to avoid the outbreak of a nuclear war. Furthermore, the outbreak of nuclear war, although horrible for its destructiveness, may not involve a fundamental catastrophe. There are many uses of nuclear weapons other than a wholesale attack on the enemy, which, in fact, appears to offer the fewest strategic rewards and thus seems highly unlikely to take place.[38] Lesser uses of nuclear weapons, although seriously disruptive of human values and sensibilities, would not inflict greater damage on mankind than have other disasters in history such as plagues or major non-nuclear wars. Such a comment does not intend to minimize the dangers of the existing situation but merely to restore some sense of proportion. A loss of poise in the face of impending hazard deepens the hazard. It is known that panic more than flames accounts for death when a fire breaks out in a crowded theater or restaurant.

It is finally relevant to observe that nuclear weapons perform a valuable restraining service, discouraging nations from taking provocative risks to promote their interests. The threat of nuclear war deters all recourse to international violence, since nuclear actors seem well aware of escalation threats that are implicit within the context of limited wars.[39]

5. The Stability of Nuclear Deterrence Is Not Automatic

There is a widespread assumption that when a nation possesses bombs big enough to destroy the cities of a potential enemy it has achieved a maximum arsenal of weapons. Anything more is opposed as unnecessary and senseless, perhaps reflecting the demonic influence of industrialists and professional soldiers who have a vested interest in the magnitude and intensity of the arms race. The assumption of this critical view is that when a nation has enough bombs to destroy an enemy it has no reason to fear attack from anyone else, and thus it has done as much in the way of nuclear defense as it is entitled to do. This presupposes the invariant capacity to deliver missiles to their targets in the event of an enemy attack. This position, widely held by humane citizens, emphasizes the over-kill capacity of present weapons to oppose the resumption of nuclear testing and the further stockpiling and proliferation of nuclear weapons and belittles the importance of inspection as an aspect of a test-ban treaty.

This assumption of automatic deterrence overlooks the continuing competition for technological improvements and break-throughs in nuclear weaponry to perfect and interfere with delivery communications systems and missile sites, lighten warheads relative to payloads, better warning and detection systems, and develop a missile defense.[40] The stability of deterrence depends on a continuing capacity to deter, which depends upon a continuing willingness to respond to and anticipate challenges created by a potential enemy's developing technology. For if a missile defense should make a nation virtually invulnerable to nuclear attack, then it can take many more provocative risks in the promotion of its foreign policy objectives. It is not only the increased tenability of nuclear warfare itself, as perceived by the advantaged state, but also the indirect tendency to worry less about the outbreak of war and more about increases in power, wealth, and prestige in various arenas of conflict. The disadvantaged state must either acknowledge the power shift occasioned by the technological break-through or hold firm despite its failure to possess weapons that constitute a credible deterrent. The rate of obsolescence in the nuclear arms race is phenomenally high. This means that blanket opposition to research and development of nuclear weaponry amounts almost to a disguised advocacy of nuclear disarmament. Thus the arguments against unilateralism apply here; in addition, reliance for defense upon a frozen state of nuclear technology involves serious self-deception that deprives the position of any possible moral dignity. Atmospheric testing of nuclear weapons often induces dogmatic opposition from those that misunderstand the nature of nuclear deterrence, calculating the deterrent effect by the ratio between stockpiled megatonnage and the explosive power needed to devastate potential target areas.

In contrast to such a mechanical approach to the relation between defense needs and moral prerogative, this essay supposes a more subtle balance of competing interests by decision-makers. The decision to conduct nuclear tests must take account of developing defense needs, radiation hazards to present and future generations, impacts on and objections of non-nuclear nations and international organizations, interferences with freedom of the seas and the airways, and the over-all consequences of testing for the maintenance of peace, the inhibition of aggression, and the growth of world order.[41]

The main consideration, then, is that a realistic approach to moral justification must reject the notion that the mere possession of nuclear weapons assures the continued presence of an automatic deterrent to a potential nuclear aggressor. If we wish to option out of the arms race for moral or political reasons, then it should be made plain what is proposed and what is to be done. This assertion, of course, does not touch upon the highly relevant moral inquiry into what rate and level of nuclear development is necessary and justifiable for an adequate continuing defense system. Such an inquiry, crucial as it is for decisions on testing and appropriations, depends upon classified information that is unavailable to the civilian population. We must rely upon the informed wisdom of our highest leaders, imploring a due regard for supranational as well as national interests. Part of the premise here is that national and supranational interests tend to converge whenever the use of nuclear force is contemplated. Thus the nation and the various levels of international organization are joined by a network of common interests. Unfortunately, the perception of overlap lags as a consequence of the persisting hold of national myths on the popular consciousness.

6. The Insufficiency of National Interest as a Principle of Justification

The assertion made here is that national decisions involving the use of nuclear force in international affairs should take cognizance of interests wider than the welfare of the state that is contemplating action. The interdependence of the modern world, especially in the context of nuclear weapons, implies a comparable broadening of the base of moral consciousness.[42] Since such a view of world affairs pervades this essay, there is no need for special elaboration at this stage.

The welfare of the national community undoubtedly enters into any pattern of adequate justification for the use of force. The claim here is simply that such a determination is not sufficient. Considerations of stability, supranational consensus, and deference to relevant regional and international organizations are additionally pertinent. Except for the narrow occasion of self-defense against a sustained armed attack across a frontier, there seems to be almost no appropriate occasion for an autonomous national decision to use force in international relations. Supranational cooperation of some sort appears essential even in the case of indirect uses of force such as military aid to a foreign government faced with an internal revolt or an external threat. At least we can expect the legitimate government to make a public request when external military support exceeds normal requirements.

Sovereignty is as morally obsolete as it is factually inaccurate. Nations depend on one another to satisfy economic and military needs. The formation of bloc and regional groupings manifests the tendency of states to overcome a heritage of national autonomy. Furthermore, this tendency should infiltrate into the search for a justification adequate to account for the uses of force, especially nuclear force.

7. Decisions to Use Nuclear and Non-Nuclear Force—A Qualitative Distinction

There is a morally significant difference between the decisions to use nuclear and non-nuclear force; this assumes that an intrinsic and symbolic gravity attaches to the use of nuclear weapons that is independent of their explosive magnitude or the damage that they may inflict upon a particular occasion. We find that the use of atomic bombs at Hiroshima and Nagasaki dominates our imagination despite the greater damage done by fire bombs at Tokyo.[43] This seems to be a rational distinction based upon the potentiality of nuclear weapons to inflict vast—if not limitless—damage, compared with other weapons (except perhaps some new varieties of bacteriological, radiological, and chemical warfare that characteristically can be kept from raising the level of destruction above what is tolerable).

The position here stated repudiates the claim that the crucial distinction is between tactical and strategic nuclear weapons, not between conventional and nuclear. There is a prevailing tendency for American military policy to assimilate tactical nuclear weapons into its plans for "conventional" or "limited" warfare.[44] This view emphasizes that the military objectives of tactical nuclear weapons used in combat situations are not outside the traditional scope of conventional warfare. Thus the qualitative decision brought about by nuclear technology only arises when the use of strategic nuclear weapons against such distant targets as enemy industry, population centers, and missile sites is contemplated. We reject this line of thinking because of our appraisal of the increased risks of escalation, Nth-Crew dispersion, and failures of command and control,[45] as well as the lack of necessity and the inability of the public to grasp the distinction between tactical and strategic weapons.

8. Particularization of Inquiry: Specific Appraisal versus Abstract Prohibition

At the same time, we must remain morally sensitive to the enormous loss of life and other values that has resulted from recent conventional wars.[46] With the obsessive scepter of nuclear war ever present, there arises a complacent inclination to regard pre-nuclear belligerency as mild and trivial. In this connection, also, we should not overlook the fact that "nuclear parity functions as an instrument of peace,"[47] discouraging as it does conduct likely to provoke violence by a potential enemy nation.

There exists a need to identify the facts of technique, provocation, objective, and intensity involved in a particular use of force in order to assess its legal and moral quality. Illegality and legality are not discrete designations, but evaluative ranges that must be made precise by the observation of a series of specific variables. Thus we are interested in the relative degree of illegality, as well as the crude characterization of an action as illegal. The ascription of a special gravity to the use of nuclear weapons is a central example of a factor (nuclearity) that controls an evaluation of relative legality and illegality. In this sense we would say that the use of non-nuclear force in the Suez by the French, British, and Israelis during the 1956 invasion was "illegal," but much less so than if nuclear weapons had been used.

II

Law and Morality in the
Context of Force

It is naïveté, not sophistication, to believe that the
conviction statesmen and nations profess and the
justifications they urge in defense of their actions
have no effect on the policies they pursue.
— ROBERT W. TUCKER[1]

It may often not be possible to do more than to clarify the
factors pointing to the legality or illegality of a particular use
of force as guides for those called upon to keep their conduct
within "the law." Thus India's attack on Goa might have an
indeterminate legal status, depending upon whether we consider the enclave as part of Portugal or as an unassimilated
part of India. The use of military force by Italy against San
Marino would pose a different problem from the use of similar force against France. The norms of international law primarily restrict the use of national force against targets that
possess international personality. No one would question, for
instance, the *international* right of the United States Government to use force to coerce the will of, say, Arkansas.
Whether to view Goa as more like Portugal or Arkansas is an
act of judgment for which we can provide scientific reasons
but cannot prevision a scientific conclusion.

The assessment of legality, which is problematic for any
legal order, is especially so for the international order. What
do we mean by characterizing conduct as "legal" or "illegal"?

The possibilities of adversary process and the presence of complementary structures of legal norms suggest that challenged action can simultaneously be described as legal and illegal, depending upon the doctrinal line of argument adopted.[2] However, the complementary structure of the legal order should not be understood as a criticism of law as a technique of social control. Complementary norms develop in response to the reality of complementary interests. Facts do not guide our interpretation to an easy distinction between what is permitted by the common interest and what is prohibited by a legal norm. Nations have a genuine interest in the use of force (self-defense) as well as in its prohibition (aggression). The decentralized character of international relations makes it peculiarly difficult to achieve an authoritative interpretation of which is which. It also establishes a situation in which an actor can invoke a norm that is favorably related to the preferred outcome. This is not necessarily sinister contempt for law. The frequency of substantial dissents from the judgments of the United States Supreme Court illustrates how difficult it is for reasonable men in a single culture to agree upon what the law requires in a specific instance.

A use of force may be described as "aggression," "self-defense," or "reprisal"; internal violence may be described as a matter of "domestic jurisdiction" or an issue of "international concern." The characterization may be used to express the outcome sought by the actor. Thus the Algerian rebels stressed the international impact of their war against the French Army, whereas the government insisted upon its domestic quality. The difference in characterization controls the status of a use of force in international law, the participation of supranational institutions, the application of the rules of war, and many other things as well. How is an impartial judge to determine which set of norms to apply?

There is a tradition in recent Anglo-American jurisprudence of stressing the indeterminacy of legal outcome from the logical point of view. This reacts against the artificial supposition, earlier so dominant in legal thinking, that the certainty and objectivity of law were guaranteed by the logical relationship between the scope of the rule and the controversial facts to which it is said to apply. This logical assurance is undercut if contradictory norms simultaneously apply with equal logical force to identical facts. This has led legal philosophers to emphasize the element of choice that must enter into any determination of legal status. It also puts emphasis upon the decisional situation. This focus highlights the value and policy dimensions that arise in the course of selecting a governing norm. If logic does not supply the criterion of decision, then it seems desirable to use the unavoidable discretion of the judge to reach the decision that most closely accords with community standards of welfare. After all, law does not exist for its own sake, but to promote the ends of society. This does not set the judge free to embark on a course of policy that is personally amenable to his sense of public good regardless of past experience. For one thing, the expectations of the community as to outcome should be satisfied if at all possible, as the predictable quality of legal status is one of the things that enables men to plan their lives. This introduces an altogether proper conservative bias into the workings of the legal process. Also there are objective methods available to determine the policies that should govern the legal inquiry. The substitution of policy for logic as a prime criterion for decision-making expands the horizon of relevance rather than personalizes the legal process. It requires a judge to look at the social consequence of alternative decisions, rather than at the logical relations between doctrine and facts.

This view of law as a process of decisions about social policy also leads to a critical distinction between casual observers and authorized decision-makers.[3] We wish to know who the appropriate decision-maker is, as well as the content of applicable legal doctrine. Is anyone other than an authoritative decision-maker capable of rendering a legal determination? In a structured domestic society it is easier to identify the authoritative decision-makers than it is in the international order, where often there is no assured forum within which to establish conduct as illegal. For example, Communist China and the United States offer contradictory legal interpretations of each other's participation in the internal wars of Southeast Asia. We would not want to identify the legal status of this conduct with the assertions of either partisan; that would be like confusing the differing roles of lawyer and judge in the adversary process. We seek to identify law with the analysis of facts, policies, and doctrine that is made by any impartial observer, regardless of whether this accords with the determinations of an authoritative decision-maker.[4] Thus, for instance, if state A complains about a use of force by B, it is possible to offer a legal appraisal of that use of force even if the appraisal appears to disagree with the judgment of the authoritative decision-maker. The participation of the United States in the invasion of Cuba in 1961 may be regarded as "illegal" even though the relevant organs of the United Nations have consistently refused to characterize the conduct of the United States as such. Law is not necessarily what the authoritative decision-maker says it is. An observer, by using evidence, policy, and norms, is independently capable of assessing legal status. Although the decisional situation provides a crucial focus for study and description, the decisions of the authorized officials do not provide our deepest insights into the application of law to life. The legal order is not an autonomous undertaking; rather it is subject to reasoned criticism from a variety of metalegal perspectives.

This argument about "legality" should take note of three separate aspects of the problem, even though thought and experience ignore the separation. First, the status of conduct as legal or illegal depending upon the perspective of the assessor as partisan, authoritative decision-maker, or scholarly observer. Second, the appraisal of the legal result, however reached, as just or unjust. And third, the relation between law and justice that is implied by a decision to obey an unjust law or to disobey a just law. This third point needs elaboration. It is not perhaps the law that is just or unjust, but its application to a set of circumstances. For instance, to choose a relevant example, rules against forcible interference in national communities are not unjust *per se*, but if their application renders weak states vulnerable to subversive take-over, then adherence to the rule may involve the infliction of a net injustice.

There is a need to confront the problem of civil disobedience in international affairs.[5] We are conscious, all too conscious, of violations of international law, but there is almost no systematic effort to provide a criterion by which to distinguish justifiable and unjustifiable illegality in international affairs. The quest for stable limits, made urgent in this time of nuclear weapons, certainly gives some value to adherence to law, particularly law dealing with coercion, for its own sake. But how much value? We do not want to argue for the absoluteness of law's claim over national or supranational discretion. There exists a need for a disciplined consideration of this matter.

This suggests the linked problem of the relation between individual and collective behavior with respect to law and morals. When an official decides, on behalf of the United

States, to violate international law it is different from a decision to violate domestic law and, as well, different from a decision by an individual to violate the law for private reasons. For a nation is *a* unit in the international system, not *the* unit as it is in the domestic system. Furthermore, an individual in his official capacity is an agent restricted to action in accordance with applicable law. Ordinary circumstances, at least in democratic society, give law supremacy within official realms of conduct. Exceptional circumstances, however, seem to authorize official lawlessness as a response to the prior claim to serve the public good.[6] That is, law is subordinate to an extraordinary criterion of welfare mediated through the conscience of the responsible official. There is one other observation: The public good should not be identified exclusively with national welfare when conduct has an international character. A national official acting in international affairs represents the interests of his state, of other states, of international society, and of mankind. The claim of national interest, no matter how well substantiated, does not provide self-sufficient support for conduct that is otherwise illegal. It may not even justify conduct that is legal.

It is useful to distinguish between a legitimation of and a justification for the use of international force. Legitimacy refers to the legal status of a use of force.[7] Justification refers to a demonstration that a given legal status corresponds with relevant moral requirements. For instance, United States military intervention to establish a democratic government in a Latin American country *might* be justifiable although it would be illegal. In contrast, a nuclear counter-strike in retaliation against a nuclear surprise attack would appear to be legal although it might not be justifiable.[8] This analytic distinction seeks to point at two different aspects of a single phenomenon. It should not, then, be read as a separation of levels of explanation. For it is a main contention of this essay that contemporary world affairs tend increasingly to unify the conditions that satisfy the claims of legitimacy and justification, and that, in fact, the failure to perceive this unity is a serious and dangerous deficiency of most national approaches to international law.[9]

An *essential* component of legitimacy is justification and a *usual* component of justification is legitimacy.[10] Since justification is treated as essential to legitimacy, it is correct to identify this essay as being in the natural-law tradition.[11]

Force is itself a neutral energy.[12] Its value or disvalue arises from the motives, prudence, and consequences of its use. There is no way to banish force from the human condition. John Dewey put this well when he said: "Not to depend upon and utilize force is simply to be without a foothold in the real world."[13] Major changes in human affairs take place when there is a significant and effective shift in the locus of discretion with regard to the use of force.[14] The formulation of a new rule relocating authority to use force must be accompanied by steps that permit effective implementation. We note that domestic social orders have effectively centralized discretion to use force in political institutions allowing only a narrow exception for self-defense in situations of severe threat from an assailant. Once discretion is centralized, the problem becomes the discovery of limits. Procedural due process seeks to achieve this result within a democratic society. Arguments against capital punishment partly seek to confine the discretion of centralized decision-makers by placing a ceiling upon the permissible application of force by the government.

The international society, in the form of institutions and rules, now also makes extensive claims over the discretion of a nation to use force. Despite these claims, however, the effective control over the use of force remains on a national level and governs the expectations and behavior of the participating units in world affairs. We should not, however, overlook how far the Charter of the United Nations purports to go in the direction of centralizing discretion over the use of force.[15] But the formulation of rules in the Charter is not enough. For the weakness of central international institutions is such that the rules are neither assured impartial interpretation nor effective application. Effective centralizations of control over the use of force involve three basic conditions: formulation of rules and standards for their interpretation, mechanisms to achieve impartial interpretation, and techniques designed to secure enforcement of impartial interpretations. Legal order is not adequately established until each condition is satisfied.

Force in human affairs is not a crude phenomenon to be identified with physical strength. It is best conceived as a spectrum that ranges from mild forms of intimidation to intense applications of violence.[16] Too often, force in international affairs is identified today only with a full-scale nuclear war. Attention must be given to threats to use force[17] and to lesser modes of coercion, and especially, in the world as we find it, to a series of interventionary techniques that usually fall short of direct military action.[18] Considerations of legitimacy and justification must be correlated with the relevant level of force. Analysis is otherwise deceptively crude, generating blanket endorsements or proscriptions of the use of force. The moral subtlety of these problems as they exist in world affairs today casts deep suspicion upon any set of conclusions that achieves a set of assured and forthright recommendations.[19] However, the difficulty of achieving a clear sense of direction should not inhibit attempts to understand and appraise the practical and moral dilemmas posed by the dispersion of nuclear technology. Neither should it lead to bland subservience to the official doctrines of the day. The

formulation of reasoned and principled alternatives, no matter how radical, provides officials and citizens with a more
illumined context for decision. Uncertainty of conclusion re-
bukes dogmatism, not radicalism. Our survival and welfare
depend upon the capacities of nations and governing groups
to have the courage and imagination to transform the world
into a different kind of political structure. This is a radical
desideratum and presupposes a willingness to think, feel, and
act in a framework that transcends attributes of our present
world.

Moral questions arise whenever humans rely upon the use
of force. This is the case whether our concern is the discipline
of children, the treatment of crowds and criminals, or the behavior of nations. How does the quality of the weapon used to
inflict or threaten violence affect the moral status of a use of
force? Does the greater magnitude of destruction that might
attend a nuclear war change the moral basis for fighting such
a war? It is desirable to avoid a morality that relies upon
weights and measures, but the troublesomeness of these
questions, at least for those who meditate upon the horror of
nuclear war, suggests that we do not understand the moral
significance of nuclear weaponry.

Force, we recall, is available as a means to achieve social
ends. Its acceptability as a means depends partly upon the
value of the end exceeding the cost of getting there. There
must be a favorable proportion between the costly consequences of the use of force and the beneficial reasons for its
use in order to make its use rational, let alone moral. Magnitude of force, then, bears upon the status of a proposed use of
force by increasing commensurately the demands for justification. However, despite the rhetoric of proportionality we
have no adequate way to quantify, or otherwise render precise, the relation between the cost of and the benefit from the

use of force. Therefore, our moral agency leads us to make intuitive distinctions that emphasize the continuing need to justify force by some sense of the cost-benefit relationship. The great damage to persons and property that would arise from a nuclear war imprecisely points, then, to the unprecedented burden of justification that must be made by a moral user of nuclear force. The moral inquiry is thus primarily a matter of rationality in the first instance, for an awareness of the relative losses that would most likely follow from such an inquiry in international affairs underscores further the moral ambiguity of the modern situation. It would be impossible to carry through a comparative analysis far enough to know whether force should be used on a particular occasion and, if so, how much.

Such an incapacity, wherein it exists, has radical consequences for a moral posture. If we are unable to ascertain whether proposed uses of forces will produce a net benefit, then we must consider whether to refrain from the use of force so long as we lack adequate justification. We do claim that adequate justification is the essential quality of a moral policy about the use of force. This leads us to accept, at least, the limited contribution that we can expect reason to make to the development of a moral policy toward the use of force.

This brief depiction of a possible approach prompts now an attempt at a more concrete definition of the problems of international force in the light of historical, social, political, and military trends and conditions. Adlai Stevenson's opening remark in the December, 1961, Security Council debate about India's invasion of Goa—"When acts of violence take place between nations in this dangerous world, no matter where they occur or for what, there is reason for alarm"[20]—sets the tone for the inquiry that follows in the next chapter.

III

The International Tableau: A Double Burden of Challenge

> Because of the potential destructiveness of modern strategic forces, the avoidance rather than the winning of war has become the first-priority objective of the Department of Defense.
>
> —HERMAN KAHN[1]

In general, there exist two authorizations for the sustained use of governmental force in international affairs. First, a government may use force to repress internal protest movements that use illegal means to achieve their objectives. The principle of legitimacy endows a government with the capacity to defend itself against indigenous and interventionary revolutionary activity that is directed against it. The issue here is more complicated if the legitimate government provides no means for its citizenry to achieve peaceful changes or if it bases its legitimacy upon a colonial or racist claim of right. It may be desirable to insist that legitimacy presupposes certain minimum conditions of fairness and morality. But if international relations are viewed from a system level, then the government in power achieves at least *de facto* legitimacy that justifies force to suppress internal threats to its supremacy.

Second, a government threatened from without by an armed attack across its borders by a foreign enemy is entitled to use sufficient defensive force to protect its territorial in-

tegrity and political independence. This authorization applies
to any national unit vis-à-vis any other national unit or combination thereof. However, the right to use defensive force
grows more ambiguous if a supranational unit is the alleged
attacker. Suppose, for instance, the United Nations eventually
mounts an armed attack against the Republic of South Africa
in order to protect the fundamental human rights of the non-
white population. Is there a right of self-defense that justifies
armed resistance to the claims of a supranational community
expressed through its relevant institutions? Momentarily, we
shall avoid giving an answer to this question, which is a novel
by-product of the increasing role played by supranational actors in conflict resolution.

Let us return now to our central concern with the status of
defensive uses of force by nations. We find an almost universal willingness to approve the use of defensive force
against foreign nations that initiate armed attacks. A state, in
other words, can rely on force to protect its survival even
though this reliance may happen to cause destruction disproportionate to the value of its independent existence.

These authorizations of defensive force in international affairs arise from an acknowledgment of the integrity of national units and from an acceptance of the internal sovereignty of governmental elites. There is no attempt to qualify
the use of force by a judgment about the nature of the society
that is being defended. Thus the propriety of governmental
uses of force derives from the basic rules that apply equally
to liberal democracies and totalitarian regimes. The basis of
self-defense is the right to defend existence *per se* rather than
the value of the self that is being defended. This distinction
contributes the primary justification for the use of nuclear
force in international affairs. And as a pattern of justification
it generates, as we shall see, corresponding legal rules.

Returning to our suspended question, we notice that the issues are somewhat different when the use of force is for, by, or against supranational units. Here the internal sovereignty of the national government is subject to certain overriding claims by wider communities of mankind.[2] This is a controversial area, expressing a state of institutional and ethical transition. It has received increasing prominence, most notably in African affairs, as the United Nations takes coercive measures to influence the outcome of various intra-societal conflicts, siding often with the antigovernmental faction. What is the scope of self-defense in these situations? When is the United Nations entitled to initiate an armed attack against a national community to achieve the goals of the organization? Norms of authorization and limitation are vague. We refer to this kind of international force to distinguish its status in law and morality from the use of force by national communities in their relations with one another.

There are also problems that arise from the use of force to defend national communities other than one's own from armed attack. Here, the principle of self-defense is collectivized to authorize a state to come to the aid of any nation that is the victim of an armed attack or a foreign intervention. The position taken here is that this kind of defensive force must rest upon a justification that is additional to a state's right to preserve its own existence. For instance, collective self-defense may firstly join together national societies that accept the same culture or same form of government or possess a degree of supranational integration to fulfill common economic or geographical objectives. Regionalism expresses the moral and political basis for collective self-defense. Perhaps even more important than bonds of regional solidarity is the generalized commitment to oppose aggressive uses of force in world affairs. It is in this spirit, for instance, that the

United States joined to resist the armed attack upon Egypt in 1956 by such primary allies as France and the United Kingdom. The commitment to minimum order properly overrides other more pervasive, but less crucial, allegiances between nations. The United States and the Soviet Union have a greater interest, it is felt, in stabilizing the conditions under which force may be used in international affairs than in emphasizing their competitive pursuit of national prestige, power, and wealth. For these reasons the United States was correct to condemn the Suez invasion even though it might have received certain immediate political benefits from its success.

It is important that the United States articulate the basis upon which it is willing to contribute to the defense force of a foreign nation either to help it repel an external attack or suppress an internal revolt. For the articulation, if relevant to conduct, helps to relate power to expectations in world affairs, giving guidance and specifying restraint. Part of the search for world order is satisfied by the establishment of common standards that help officials to distinguish between permissible and impermissible uses of nuclear force.

The United States faces a double challenge to its survival: totalitarian encroachment and nuclear devastation. The risks of the age burden us with the moral necessity to meet both challenges, although meeting one too ardently leads to an increased vulnerability to the other. Consider, for instance, the antitotalitarian advantages of intervention in East Europe as offset by the risk of triggering a nuclear war. Or consider the increase in safety that would result from a unilateral destruction of nuclear weapons as weighed against the danger of Communist expansion in the uncommitted nations, especially in Asia and Latin America, and the use of blackmail techniques to gain ascendency elsewhere. It is the necessity to

balance national responses to such challenges as these that
creates the distinctive moral as well as the political crisis of
our age. Great tension arises from the prospect of a single or
double failure. It is this necessity that excites extreme domestic anxiety, articulated by such groups as the John Birch
Society or the various peace-marching organizations. The
formulation of rational policy depends upon our continuing
capacity to resist distortions that arise from fear.

It is a subsidiary moral requirement that we distinguish
anti-totalitarianism from anti-Communism. Communism today constitutes the most powerful and menacing expression
of totalitarianism, but there exist also non-Communist and
anti-Communist authoritarian and totalitarian regimes that
coerce individuals with relentless ruthlessness. Our moral
stand against such political groupings should not disappear
under the pressure of the Communist challenge. It may be
prudent to cooperate with these friendly authoritarian and
totalitarian societies in order to strengthen our defenses
against the Soviet bloc. This may, for instance, justify the ad-
mission of Spain and Portugal to NATO, but it should not be
allowed to confuse the moral grounds for the use of force in
world affairs. Alliance with totalitarian governments is, perhaps, an expression of moral ambiguity of political life, but it
should never become more than this. The enthusiasm of some
rightist groups for Tshombe's Katanga just because it adopted
anti-Communist slogans suggests the dangers that arise from
a loss of moral clarity about what challenges and what expresses our way of life. We must learn to distinguish sharply
between the political necessity of selective cooperation with
nations that are dominated by unacceptable systems and our
moral approval of them. It is certainly wrong to conceive of
international politics as a struggle between the forces of good
("we") and evil ("they"). Often a national community is

compelled to choose between evils. Our cooperation with the Soviet Union in World War II to defeat Hitler was an occasion when United States support for a totalitarian society in war was quite justified. But the justification for support does not imply approval of that which is supported. In this sense the *Realpolitik* tradition spares us the painful reversals of national attitude that we experienced after World War II with regard to West Germany and the Soviet Union. For realists regard international relations as a struggle to make responsible uses of national power and so to maximize national interests; moral categories are irrelevant to such an endeavor. The decisive objection to this approach is that it refuses to acknowledge the claims of morality in the field of political action, thereby making political decisions overly subject to pragmatic calculations.

There must also exist a willingness to acknowledge antitotalitarian changes within Communist national societies and perhaps within the Communist system as a whole. At the same time we must be on guard against wishful interpretations of internal changes in antagonistic totalitarian societies. Liberalizations may have significant value from a humanitarian viewpoint, as when political prisoners are released from jail, without changing the coercive character of the regime; as well, changes may be temporary, soon to be reversed by a return to the more oppressive patterns of the past. Thus while it is probably essential to realize the persisting significance of the seizure of power by Communist elites through the violent suppression of their opposition and to keep in mind that governmental transfers of power in Communist states still depend upon coercion rather than upon popular consent, we must also grow aware of the difference between Stalinist purges and Khrushchevian banishments.[3] We find that Albania, Poland, China, and Yugoslavia exhibit, at present, significantly distinct patterns of domestic politics despite their common ideological base in Communism. Totalitarianism is also a relative term: We must be ready to consider its severity, its capacity for change, contraction, and expansion, and its degree of internal support. Here, as with force itself, we need to think of a continuum that allows totalitarianism to shade off into non-totalitarianism rather than employ an either/or model of reality. Our physical and spiritual survival now depends more upon developing a capacity to make accommodations with non-totalitarian groupings of political power (which includes our capacity to recognize such groupings), than it does upon new weapons systems. Similarly, we must not be trapped by our own ideological preferences for private control over capital into an automatic hostility toward social systems that rely upon the public control of economic development. Democratic socialism presents a non-totalitarian political model that is consistent with the moral position outlined in this paper. An operational distinction between socialism (non-totalitarian) and Communism (totalitarian) is part of the basis urged for the use of defensive force in world politics.

The urgency of the times requires us to draw upon all our resources to resist totalitarianism and to reduce the prospect of nuclear war. A principal argument of this essay is that these resources significantly include the moral foundations of international law to an extent far greater than most have been willing to acknowledge. The claims of law to control behavior must be examined within the social and political environment of international relations. Especially, it is necessary to grasp relations among military strategy, political expansion, world order, and rules of law if we are concerned with the use of law to regulate national recourse to force. In this task the perspectives of political science and law converge as we insist upon conceiving of law within the limits of political feasibility.

However, there is an unfortunate tendency on the part of nonlegal analysts of international affairs to neglect the potential contributions of law to world order. Up until World War II, international law was either the preserve of moralists who prescribed ideal legal remedies for the ills of mankind or of botanical scholars who collected rules and instances of practice. Little attention was given to the political and social conditions that permit or resist the regulation of national behavior by the norms and processes of law. There were notable exceptions like Huber, Schindler, Alvarez, and Visscher, but the dominant image of international law was shaped by the dogmatic form of legal positivism associated mostly prominently with Kelsen or the descriptive type of legal positivism identified with Lauterpacht. Of course, there are many variants of the Kelsen and Lauterpacht approaches, but they share a presentation of legal phenomena in isolation from the international environment. Recent scholars, especially McDougal, Lasswell, Röling, Katzenbach, and Kaplan, have helped to restore an appreciation of law within the context of value and power. But their vision of the link between law and politics has not been assimilated, as yet, into the dominant patterns of thinking in the field of international relations. Thus it becomes important to demonstrate as vividly as possible that law does offer invaluable technique, procedure, and experience for those concerned with increasing the quality of international stability. In the following pages I shall try to demonstrate the relevance of law to the control of international force and the prevention of nuclear war, as well as describe the regulative impact of morality.

For one thing, the control of international force by the regulatory processes and standards of law and morality dis-

courages radical domestic groups that currently seek to narrow our destiny to a single duty: For such singleness of vision
involves either a militant disregard for the horror of nuclear
war or an evident indifference to totalitarian encroachment.
We argue here that it is essential to combine resistance to
totalitarian encroachment with a deeply serious effort to cut
the risks of general nuclear war. Explication of this double
commitment makes clearer the direction of our specific moral
responses, which, in turn, highlights the role and nature of international law with respect to decisions about the use of international force. We will briefly describe the international
situation that occasions this double response to discover more
precisely the patterns of behavior that threaten us and the
means that are available to cut the threat. Let us begin with
a brief account of the characteristics of thermonuclear warfare that so uniquely challenge the existing system of international order.

Thermonuclear technology portends a tragic destiny for
mankind.[4] Despite the seeming impossibility of assessing
probabilities, we are startled to discover that even staunch
advocates of the prevailing strategy of nuclear deterrence
concede that "the probability of a large thermonuclear war
occurring appears to be significantly larger than the probability of its not occurring."[5] It borders upon the pathological
to favor a course of action that we actively *suppose* will lead
to a breakdown of such stupefying magnitude as thermonuclear warfare. It discloses either the absence of feasible alternatives or a shocking disregard or unawareness of them.[6]
Widening support within the United States for an extensive
program of civil defense has begun to dramatize the risk of
nuclear war to the general community.[7] The risk of devastation gives rise to urgent demands for an adequate moral justification of our existing defense policies and a maximum effort

to discover policies that will cut the risks of war without impairing the essentials of military security.[8] A particular task of this inquiry is to translate the imperatives of military security into a series of tentative propositions about the legal control of international force. It is desirable to use legal techniques to objectify policy commitments, so that all national actors may perceive the boundaries of impermissible coercion and avoid unintended breakdowns of political equilibrium.[9] A guiding principle of this approach is the insistence that we reconcile legal restraints with wider normative orders. This demand for reconciliation permits us to explicate the distinction between good and bad law.[10] Our presentation likewise intends to challenge those who seem to discern the proper limits for the use of nuclear weapons in international affairs by an exclusive and rigid inquiry into the military dynamics of the Cold War. We cannot vindicate a decision or even a provisional willingness to use nuclear weapons against innocent people[11] and centers of civilization until we have developed a new morality that relates current military strategy to the new technology of the thermonuclear age.

Our nuclear preparation for war, involving unprecedented expense, seeks mainly to deter aggression by Communist nations.[12] The subleties of political expansion are such, however, that we seem reluctant to specify the conditions that would prompt us to use nuclear weapons. We retain flexibility but forgo communication. The United States has been unclear about specifying the conditions under which it will make use of nuclear weapons. In addition, the United States has shown great reluctance to accept a definition of aggression that would be available to guide national leaders and organs of the United Nations in case of a dispute about an actual or threatened use of force.[13] National policy refuses to give up its traditional discretion with respect to decisions leading to

the use of defensive force in world affairs.[14] It is true that it is
hard to negotiate a definition that does not include substantial risks of evasion. It would, however, seem possible to posit
a definition and then extend its reach to loopholes as they appear. We do this constantly with domestic regulation. No rational person would eliminate the income tax because groups
of taxpayers have from time to time found ways to avoid its
restrictive claims. It should, of course, be evident that a definition of aggression could combine specific instances with a
general clause that would permit the institution entrusted
with characterizing behavior under the definition to add new
categories of aggression to the definition as they arose. As a
nation we are slow to accept the risks of self-restriction and
hence continue to expose ourselves to the greater perils of
nonrestriction. A definition of aggression would not end the
problem of discerning impermissible uses of force in international affairs, but it would at least initiate the evolutionary
process by which mutual standards of limitation gradually
bring order into human affairs. At present, the absence of objective standards accentuates the problems posed for world
order by the refusal of states to transfer power to supranational institutions.[15]

The claim to characterize provocative action unilaterally as
"aggression" is used to support the right to use defensive
force. Such a claim overlooks the ever more interdependent
impact that any significant use of nuclear weapons has on international affairs. The traditional grant of sovereign discretion rested upon a relative condition of national independence on a factual level. We now live in a contrasting
world of predominant national interdependence, thereby
making any nation's independent power to decide appear
deeply arbitrary. There is a lag in supranational superstruc-
ture and doctrine that creates a tension between the facts of

interdependence and the persisting claims of independence. Even greater than this lag is the backwardness of collective consciousness, which continues to conceive of political reality in world affairs in the spirit of patriotism and nationalism, disregarding the minimum universalization of impact that results from the testing, possession, and use of nuclear weapons.

This new interdependence can be illustrated in several respects. First, a general nuclear war would almost certainly produce a global economic and political dislocation—far greater than the serious dislocations that accompanied the recent world wars—that would seriously threaten the survival and viability of many states not directly involved in the conflict.[16] Second, major nuclear explosions may produce lethal fallout that does not confine itself to the national boundaries of the target state. Therefore, national societies that participate neither in the provocative action nor in the decision to make a nuclear response are made indirect, but substantial, victims of a nuclear war. Thus the welfare of the world, as an indivisible community of victims, is entrusted to the calculations of a small governmental elite of a single nuclear state.[17] Third, the character of nuclear weapons is such that essential preparations for war—especially atmospheric testing of prospective weapons—inflict intense anxiety and indeterminate damage upon non-nuclear societies.[18] In this way, not only is the distinction between belligerent and nonbelligerent eliminated, but the distinction between war and peace is significantly blurred.[19] The basic limiting premises (just and unjust war; combatant and noncombatant; military and civilian targets) of the traditional patterns for justifying force thus appear to be quite obsolete under present conditions.[20] Despite the obvious aspiration of many non-nuclear states for neutrality, the global impact of nuclear warfare undermines a posture of nonparticipation.[21]

This situation both posits the claims of non-nuclear nations to participate in decisions that control their destiny[22] and calls into profound question the traditional position of the state as "sovereign" in matters touching its vital interests. Although we now regard sovereignty as qualified by a commitment to conform to applicable standards of international law, there remains a residual claim to decide the occasion for and the quantity of appropriate uses of defensive force. Freedom in such decisions expresses the continuing claim of the state to be the fundamental defensive unit in international affairs. But today the military security of a state depends upon elaborate affiliation with one or more blocs of states, each of which is itself dependent upon the overwhelming force of nuclear nations. Increasingly, also, the basic economic unit is expanding from a national economy to a regional or functional unit that includes a number of national units. Thus the nation no longer provides the military or economic conditions for the fulfillment of man's endeavor to achieve physical security and material well-being. At the same time, however, nationalistic sentiments are relied upon to arouse continuing support for the appropriation of enormous resources to the tasks of defense and foreign aid. As the orbit of conscious loyalty is set by the contours of the national boundary, there is a marked unwillingness to submit the welfare of the nation to the judgment of supranational institutions. And so it is not unexpected that traditional prerogatives of national discretion are jealously retained.

We observe, for instance, the persisting refusal of the United States to allow the International Court of Justice to decide which disputes belong within domestic jurisdiction.[23] The popular understanding of sovereignty still appears to support Morgenthau's view that "International politics can be defined as a continuing effort to maintain and increase the power of one's own nation and to keep in check or reduce the power of other nations."[24]

Yet this conception of international politics seems strikingly anachronistic in so many ways.[25] It is no longer feasible to separate an assessment of national welfare—on almost any important issue of foreign policy—from effects its resolution will have upon various communities of states more or less united (or opposed) on ideological or cultural grounds.[26] Beyond this, the danger of nuclear war is such that minimum international order—that is, some limiting condition of hostility short of nuclear warfare—creates a goal that is permanently common for all enemies so long as they perceive the graveness of the danger and do not indulge highly irrational policies.[27] We are left with dominantly nationalistic patterns of thought and practice in a world that is increasingly supranational and universal in function and need.[28] This unresolved contradiction, a consequence of the lag of collective consciousness behind the emergence of new facts, presents on the operational level insurmountable problems for decisions about legal commitment and moral justification.

The profound challenges to old ways of thought and organization created by military technology and functional interdependence exist amid severe dangers of totalitarian encroachment. The Sino-Soviet bloc possesses geopolitical advantages, ideological vigor, a record of ruthless destruction, and a rhythm of expansion and cumulative influence.[29] These developments remind us of the moral charge to choose means sufficient to meet the totalitarian challenge. Let us remember the doubleness of our burden. And so let us guard against seductive and pusillanimous pleas for recourse to policies of unilateral renunciation of nuclear weapons.[30] We confront a Cold War antagonist that is hampered by few parallel moral inhibitions. The internal history of suppression within the

Soviet Union and Red China, the Soviet response to the Hungarian uprising in 1956, Chinese cruelty in Tibet, and the irresponsible magnitude of the 1961 Soviet nuclear test series are persuasive evidence of the gravity of the menace.[31] Fear of war with the West alone seems to restrict the expansionist program of revolutionary nations like China and the Soviet Union. This validates temporarily the major premise of deterrence theory, namely, that the physical containment of the Communist bloc requires the inhibiting presence of indestructible nuclear weapons.[32]

This mandate to resist totalitarianism does not imply a Manichean interpretation of world politics. The Communist world is rather new and several of its nations appear to be evolving into non-totalitarian societies.[33] Moreover, there is much totalitarian and autocratic political practice in the non-Communist part of the world, and there are many social evils in states enjoying non-coercive forms of domestic government. Poverty, overpopulation, disease, economic exploitation, religious and racial persecution and discrimination, illiteracy, inadequate housing and sanitation, unemployment, refugee hardships, and colonial domination are present in totalitarian and nontotalitarian societies alike. The Communist opposition to some of these evils is more direct than is our own. Let us, therefore, not oversimplify the contrast between the totalitarian and nontotalitarian nations in the world, nor identify the West with an undifferentiated commitment to democratic political behavior in enjoyment of the good life. We must also seek to assess the relevance of evils other than totalitarianism to our arguments about legitimate uses of military force if we wish to achieve an adequate pattern of justification.

In like regard, it is essential that we try to appraise the relative costs of various forms of defeat in the Cold War. Norman

Podhoretz properly asks us to examine our capacity to survive surrender in the same spirit of seriousness that we adopt to inquire about the costs of nuclear war should it come to pass.[34] There is a tendency to think about "tolerable losses" only in the context of nuclear war. But what kind of losses are tolerable in the context of Communist domination? That is, how would the United States suffer in the event that the Sino-Soviet bloc actually did run our society? These questions should be withdrawn from the realm of the unthinkable by the tough-minded analyst in a manner that parallels Kahn's withdrawal of the post–nuclear-war world from that same realm.

didn't do it

The dependence of Western defenses upon nuclear weapons is most clear in Central Europe, especially in West Germany and West Berlin. However, this very dependence compels us to consider carefully alternative means, including conventional forces, arms control, and disarmament, that are available to protect the *status quo.* For we cannot fulfill our duty to avoid nuclear war unless we take all available and reasonable measures to reduce the risk of its occurrence. Thus the refusal to bolster our European capacities sufficiently to meet Soviet provocation or miscalculation with conventional weapons appears to be a serious moral delinquency on the part of the West.[35] It is incumbent upon us to use every feasible means to expand the margin between conflict and nuclear war in the event Cold War tensions lead to actual violence.[36]

An obvious way to do this is to reduce our dependence upon nuclear weapons in Europe. Such a reduction of dependence, however, appears to run counter to weapons policies now dominant in the United States. For instance, American combat troops in the Seventh Army who patrol Communist borders in Europe are reported to be equipped now with the Davy Crockett (a bazooka capable of using nuclear ammunition) at their most advanced points of contact.[37] This weapon can be operated by two men in the field; hence problems of command and control are greatly increased with regard to the decision to initiate the use of nuclear weapons. According to the newspaper account, the decision to give the Davy Crockett to front-line troops "confirms the United States adoption of a once controversial assumption: that small, tactical nuclear weapons can be used in ground hostilities without provoking a general nuclear war." Furthermore, it is assumed that "tactical nuclear weapons of this type are merely more powerful than conventional arms and should not be classed with strategic nuclear weapons."[38] Such a policy regards the qualitative weapons decision to be the initiation of strategic nuclear weapons, not just nuclear weapons. Hence it conflicts with the argument made here, which regards the crucial distinction to be between nuclear and nonnuclear weapons. Beyond this there does not seem to be any existing threat of a Soviet armed attack against any part of Western Europe that can possibly justify this decision to bring "the deadliest weapon of its size ever brought to a front-line position near hostile forces."[39] Such weapons policies seem to neglect the perils of escalation and accidental warfare to a shocking degree. Instead of attenuating the danger of unintended belligerency, we appear to be aggravating it.

Not only should we construct our policies with a minimum reliance upon nuclear weapons but we should also take more seriously, despite the risks and obstacles, proposals to establish a denuclearized zone in Central Europe. The Soviet Union would probably gain certain immediate military advantages from this type of adjustment, but the West might gain a more stable equilibrium in a situation where it presently lacks strategic flexibility.[40] At this stage of international relations the achievement of international stability is the contradiction of appeasement.[41] We must increasingly value international law for its contributions to the stability of international life rather than merely as a useful instrument of battle in the Cold War.[42] This requires, in part, a greater appreciation of what "national interest" has come to mean in the nuclear age. The serious quest for minimum world order must now proceed in diplomatic corridors as well as in utopian wildernesses. The public awareness of the broadening base of national interests appears to lag dangerously.[43] This quest, also, must be viewed in the light of the doubleness of the challenge. Although it is essential to find a universal basis for stability by the creation of norms, institutions, and procedures that are acceptable to both Cold War rivals, it is also imperative to resist the development or tolerance of a legal order that facilitates Communist expansion.[44] Such a balance is not easy to achieve, as our unfortunate sponsorship of the 1961 invasion of Cuba tends to suggest in retrospect.[45]

A central effect of the fear of nuclear war is to transform characteristic patterns of international violence from wars *between* nations to wars *within* a nation.[46] The principal extensions of political influence today arise from intervention rather than invasion. The prohibition of boundary-crossing gives some assurance that a conflict will not expand into a nuclear war. This basic stabilizing norm was reinforced by the effective United States response to boundary-crossing in Korea and Suez. It has been somewhat weakened by the successful invasions of Tibet and Goa. The Soviet Union and the United States evidently continue to adhere firmly to this limiting standard. Neither Soviet force in Hungary in 1956 nor American participation in the attempted Cuban intervention of 1961 affects the integrity of this limiting rule.

However, client wars and pervasive interventionary tactics seem to render obsolete the traditional norms of international law pertaining to nonintervention, independence, and self-determination. The Cold War, global interdependence, and the prevalence of domestic conflict in uncommitted nations set the scene for intervention. Repression, the absence of an international legislative process, and the willingness of Cold War actors to give help encourage internal protest movements to ask for external support. This often leads directly to intervention and counterintervention resulting in serious bloodshed, terror, and destruction. Such a procedure for the settlement of domestic conflict is costly and dangerous, constantly tempting the intervening nations to raise the ante when the outcome of an internal war appears adverse to one or the other Cold War bloc.

Thus the interdependent quality of world affairs today contrasts with the hypothesis of internalness that led to the formation of the old rules of noninterference. The ideal of national self-determination continues to dominate the political imagination of mankind in the less developed portions of the world. But the struggle to achieve national independence and the insistence in Africa upon creating a multitude of small nations interferes with the welfare of the inhabitants of the territory. But the irrationality of indigenous political aspirations does not render any more acceptable the willingness of the superstates to determine the outcome of a domestic conflict by a violent struggle sponsored by the rival interventions of Cold War blocs: It raises tension closer to the nuclear threshold, and it abuses the population and territory that are undergoing the struggle. However, the second imperative of moral responsibility in world affairs—the defense against totalitarian advance—prohibits the adoption of a policy of unconditional unilateral nonintervention. The survival of

Franco's Government is an unpleasant legacy of the moral and political impoverishment of a policy of absolute nonintervention by democratic nations.[47]

Between the Scylla of intervention and the Charybdis of nonintervention we search the treacherous waters for markings that raise the mariner's hope for safe passage. Several emerge.[48] First, when domestic strife takes place within a nation that is a member of a bloc, the rival bloc should adhere to a policy of rather strict nonintervention.[49] Such a policy has been followed in Guatemala (1954), Hungary, East Germany, Poland (1956), and Cuba (1961). The dangers of unmanageable conflict are so great that the duty to avoid nuclear war seems to take precedence, here, over the duty to resist totalitarianism. Second, when domestic strife takes place in a nonbloc (or uncommitted) nation, intervention by one bloc authorizes non-nuclear counterintervention by the other bloc of approximately symmetrical character.[50] This pattern finds expression especially in South Asia (for example, South Vietnam, Laos) and somewhat in the Middle East and Africa. Here, the containment of totalitarian rule ordinarily justifies the risks of violent combat. However, the intrinsic costs of bloodshed, the possibilities of escalation, and the heightening of tensions everywhere make this pattern of symmetrical counterintervention no better than a lesser evil. This leads to a third normative pattern that is the hardest to articulate and yet the most promising to contemplate: Where internal violence appears likely to induce active intervention by major nations, responsible officials in national societies should endeavor to entrust the United Nations with the job of re-establishing order. The Congo operation provides both the clearest and most problematic instance.

It is probable that a United Nations enforcement action, like effective national or collective intervention, would inter-

fere with the natural outcome of internal strife; this constitutes the cost of improving international stability. It is acceptable only if it is accompanied by an increasing willingness of
the United Nations to use nonviolent coercion (censure, economic sanctions) to compel minimum social changes in nations outside the two major blocs.[51] That is, decolonialization
(patterns of foreign domination outside of Europe) and the
elimination of the politics of racial superiority (institutional
and legal oppressions of racial or religious groups) must become an organic part of the increasing participation of the
United Nations in the domestic affairs of its members.[52] Furthermore, the United Nations must not impair its fragile prestige by attempts to stabilize domestic strife in areas that
have become Cold War arenas within which rival interventions have already taken place. For the necessity to choose
between domestic factions will lead the United Nations, at
this stage of its development, to antagonize deeply the various sponsors of the disfavored factions. The events in the
Congo have led each major nation interested in the final resolution to take positions of animated hostility toward some
aspect of the United Nations role there. Despite these problems and others, the Congo precedent furnishes a promising
alternative to the tendency of Cold War actors to choose domestic struggles as proxy battlegrounds for international
conflict.

Fourth, and finally, we find a modest trend toward regional
decision-making with regard to interventionary conduct in
the Western hemisphere. The United States now seems parti-
ally willing to act against Cuba by recourse to the formal
sanctioning measures of the Organization of American States
rather than by exclusive reliance upon unilateral measures of
illegal intervention.[53] This shift significantly acknowledges
the growing willingness to regard legitimate uses of military

coercion, except for self-defense against an actual armed attack,[54] as a matter for supranational responsibility. It is a result of present legal commitments and factual interdependencies that curtail the traditional province of unilateral claims by nations to act coercively in international affairs.

These four principles of normative restraint purport to reconcile, as much as these complex political patterns allow, the simultaneous necessities to avoid nuclear war and to resist totalitarian advance. The principles themselves, depending as they do upon mutual adherence, assert limitations that maximize security and welfare for both totalitarian and non-totalitarian nations. The legal order must not itself choose sides in the Cold War. Partisanship of this variety would diminish the actual and potential value of law's protection against uncontrollable international violence.[55] However, at the same time that we respect the neutrality of legal restraints,[56] we must not allow legal rules to operate as a Communist instrument of expansion. This requires a balancing of aspirations that is bound to fail whenever it degenerates into a mere compromise. Perhaps the clearest lesson of our participation in the Cuban intervention in 1961 was that a mechanical compromise between fidelity to legal commitments[57] and a wish to win a battle in the Cold War leads to the frustration of both objectives.[58]

Justification for normative standards depends upon fulfilling the conditions that make for a dual accommodation—a simultaneous reduction of the risk of nuclear war and a tolerance for successful participation in the Cold War. Several directions of action incline efficiently toward this end: First, a defense policy that reduces the occasions upon which military defense rests upon nuclear weapons. Second, a firm endorsement of the normative prohibition against violent crossing of international boundaries; no provocation authorizes the initiation of an armed attack across an international frontier. Third, the differentiation between intervention in domestic strife within one's own bloc and within the rival bloc (Cuba vs. Hungary), the use of symmetrical counterintervention in nonbloc internal wars, and the encouragement of increasing United Nations participation in the resolution of internal wars that have not already been drawn deeply into the Cold War. Fourth, the use of the United Nations to promote internal social changes that help attain fundamental human rights; such external pressure fulfills, in primitive fashion, the central task of an international legislature.

Bearing this analysis in mind, it is necessary now to look more narrowly at the legal control of force in international affairs and then proceed to re-examine its present grounds of justification. It should be stressed that a moral policy toward international force includes the use of significant resources to explore the prospects for disarmament and arms control.[59] We have reached the stage where the national defense system seems too costly and dangerous for *all* major actors in world affairs. This situation both threatens us with extinction and provides the rational basis for radical transformation of political organization in many areas of supranational concern.[60] Progress, however, faces many obstacles. There is one in particular that appears to be worth mentioning. To what extent does a coercive domestic pattern of politics preclude the reliable adoption of a consensual system of international control over the use of force? Can a totalitarian society sustain international cooperation with respect to the coercive instruments of power that it uses without limitation in its management of internal affairs? These questions point to certain hazards that arise when nontotalitarian national systems of power consider giving up their access to the weapons needed for their military defense. On the opposite side of the ledger we find parallel doubts. Can a nontotalitarian society composed of diverse pressure groups make a reliable decision that it will abide by that involves a fundamental change in its pattern of security and defense? If events after disarmament diminish the relative power of democratic societies, will their populations, let alone their leaders, accept the new noncoercive rules of the game? Of course, shifts in elites in nondemocratic societies pose similar questions, but somehow less pointedly.

It seems appropriate at this point to move from a depiction of the tableau of world politics to a brief account of the way in which international law seeks to regulate the use of force in international affairs.

IV

International Force
and International Law

> Paradoxical as it may seem, the fundamental con-
> ceptions of international law can best be under-
> stood if it is assumed that they maintain and
> support the rule of force.
> —GEORGE W. KEETON and
> GEORG SCHWARZENBERGER[1]

Any presentation of international law is likely to suffer from
widespread and contradictory public attitudes of cynicism
and utopianism. Many students of world affairs either discount international law altogether or expect everything from
it. It is rare indeed to encounter a just appreciation of the
limits upon and opportunities for legal order in the world today. In general, we have, in Brierly's words, an encounter between "the practical man who imagines that he has shed his
illusions, and believes quite simply that international law is a
sham" and "the ultra-legalist lawyer who deals in codes and
formulas as though they contained a magic of their own, or of
the enthusiastic layman who imagines that earnest aspiration
after a better international order can take the place of patient
study of the problems concerned."[2] Especially with respect to
the control of international force there is a tendency on the
part of observers to adopt an all-or-nothing attitude toward
international law. This introductory remark seeks only to
warn cynics and utopians against the text that follows and

to reproach them for their refusal to allow the realities of the ongoing system of international law to inform their vision of its shortcomings, achievements, and prospects.

We can begin to understand the relation of law and force in international affairs only if we take the distinctive character of the international legal system into account. This requires an appreciation of the horizontal distribution of authority, the bipolar concentration of power, and the ineffectiveness of vertical institutions and procedures for the development of international legal order.[3] Domestic society relies upon effective vertical concentration of authority and power to compel its members to accept normative restraints. The solidarity of most domestic societies creates spontaneous community support for most legal standards; furthermore, a domestic society possesses adequate mechanisms for change should this support disappear. Prohibition and anti-segregation norms illustrate the difficulties of enforcing law that arouses community hostility and civil strife even in a well-organized democratic society. These difficulties are compounded in international society where nations maintain the dominant tradition that the simultaneous pursuit of national interest by the countries of the world presupposes patterns of conflict more than structures of cooperation. There is an objective basis for this tradition. One must question, however, the tradition in the light of the new prospect of thermonuclear devastation and the claim of one power center to revolutionize the world.[4] There is far less harmony in international society where national units have a tradition of selfish and antagonistic pursuits of wealth and power. Cultural diversity, economic disparity, and imperial designs are certainly among the basic historical explanations of international violence.[5] Also, the international society does not possess effective techniques for the pacific settlement of conflicts and disputes. In particular, conflicts that arise from contradictory aspirations for wealth, power, and prestige cannot be adjusted very easily by existing supranational mechanisms. India's invasion of Goa in 1961 and Algerian insurgency from 1954 onward are recent illustrations of recourse to force as the exclusive means to reach a political result that was in agreement with the overwhelming consensus of world opinion.

It is not only a matter of inadequate supranational techniques for the promotion of social change; it is the national possession and retention of the means for violent resolution of conflicts that unsettles international life. In domestic societies there is no normal residuum of private violence available for the pursuit of grievances not satisfied by the institutions of the state. Self-help, except in situations of rebellion and anarchy, is virtually eliminated from the domestic scene. In a sense, the central problem of world order is to achieve a comparable elimination of self-help from the international scene.

But our primary interest is to look at what international law presently contributes to the control of force, not what must be done to make international control as adequate as domestic control. There are special difficulties for international law generated by the distinctive quality of contemporary politics. For instance, we find the central normative distinction between "war" and "peace" in traditional international law incompatible with the factuality of the Cold War.[6] This dramatizes the need for the development of normative categories that can accommodate the wide range of techniques by which and objectives for which force is used in international affairs. It is obviously a crude system that tends to classify "nonrecognition" and "an armed attack" as instances of "intervention" despite the discretionary status of recognition and the forbidden nature of aggressive military operations.[7] This need to particularize inquiry into a contested or proposed use of force is a fundamental aspect of adequate analysis, although it is difficult to achieve because of the poverty of normative resources of traditional international law. This makes it crucial to give a precise description of the facts so that we will not be led to assume the legal equivalence of dissimilar patterns of conduct just because they are put into a single doctrinal category. The entire notion of horizontal legal order is an attempt to expand the normative and institutional resources of the international system.

These problems stem partly from modern developments. The prohibitive costs of general warfare between nuclear blocs put a premium upon the pursuit of national objectives by lesser modes of coercion. This contrasts with the historical obsession with the regulation of military operations across recognized international frontiers that attain a sufficiently sustained pattern to warrant the characterization of "war." This emphasis on war reflected the concern of political actors, and provided as well the focus of inquiry for international jurists. Sophisticated students of international law are sceptical about claiming that law controls coercion that is less than war. The distinguished Danish internationalist, Alf Ross, suggests that "it will be wisest to let the chapter on intervention disappear entirely from International Law, at any rate for the present. For here we have passed the limit of what has a reasonable chance of being respected as law."[8] Ross goes on to say:

> In principle, intervention is violence as part of the policy of states. To stretch expectation too far on this point by pretending that the law can forbid any such thing is merely to undermine the confidence in International Law in a sphere where it really might mean something.[9]

This view has great significance. International law should extend its claims to control on the basis of notions of effectiveness, not wishful thinking. However, in dissent from Ross, it is felt that law can usefully clarify standards pertaining to intervention and thereby reduce the risks of unintended escalation that might otherwise be present when interventionary politics become tainted with Cold War rivalries. It may be helpful to precede a description of the relation between international law and intervention in internal affairs by a short sketch of the main juridical attempts to restrain the use of force in international affairs.

Medieval attempts to restrict the use of force by the specification of moral criteria failed to dissuade nations from conquest. The development of the Just War doctrine, under the sway of Christian moral philosophy, was able neither to discourage violence nor to mobilize the collective force of the community against the unjust breaker of the peace.[10] Gradually jurisprudential concern shifted from efforts to control recourse to belligerency to the development of techniques for the limitation of ensuing hostilities.[11] Therefore, writers emphasized rules governing nonparticipation (neutrality) and restricting the cruelty of war (law of war). In the nineteenth century, especially, it became clear that political methods were alone able to restrict recourse to force. Thus the balance-of-power system, in its favorable aspect, sought to confront any potential aggressor with enough defensive force to discourage aggression. There was no serious attempt to condemn the recourse to force as itself illegal or even wrong.[12] In fact, the acceptance of auto-interpretation effectively allowed each belligerent to attribute justice to his own use of force, and this attribution was not subject to revision by the collective judgment of the community of nations or by the impartial judgment of a neutral nation or a panel of experts. The doctrine of sovereignty insulated auto-interpretation from objective review by a secular agency; national decisions were reviewable only in the light of their compatibility with divine ordinance, and then only by the monarch or the ruling elite within the actor's government. It is hardly necessary to observe that such a regime of auto-interpretation rarely arrives at the conclusion that a use of international force is "illegal" or "unjust."[13] For nations, like individuals, are loathe to make public self-condemning judgments about their conduct and strive instead to rationalize their behavior by an appeal to some kind of justification, however dubious it may appear to bystanding actors. War, then, operated in the international system as the most intense political technique available to a state for the pursuit of national goals. From a systemic perspective, recourse to war had no legal status. More significantly, the fruits of successful conquest were incorporated into a legally valid peace treaty that bound the victim state even if its consent was obtained by duress: "The international law of peace has for three centuries stabilized the equilibrium achieved by force in the fundamental peace treaties concluded since 1648."[14]

This tolerance of war and the ratification of its results does, up to this day, make the claims of international law as law appear problematic to many observers of the international scene. For if a state is entitled to wage war against another state it seems artificial to hold it responsible for all the lesser delinquencies that excite jurists, such as failures to respect the immunity of diplomats. Why should a state worry about its duty to respect the innocent passage of foreign vessels through its territorial waters if it is entitled to wage a war of conquest against any foreign state? Logic misleads here. It is correct to observe the folly of insisting upon the legal control of lesser violations of national rights in contrast to the lawless status of the greatest violations, but it points only to the hazard of the system, not its nonexistence. For the normal condition of international relations leads all states to seek a reliable set of standards to govern the wide variety of international transactions. These standards are most conveniently created and sustained within a normative environment that uses the rhetoric and techniques of law. It is to this extent a functioning legal order, despite its inability to exert fully effective control over resort to violence. Up to the present time, nations have insisted upon the capacity to use force as a continuing and ultimate alternative to the inhibitions placed upon national freedom by the normative restraints that make up international law.

To gain confidence in international law as law we must identify the distinctive elements and aims of international legal order. International law rests upon a generalized preference for order in *all* international relationships *most* of the time and order in *some* international relationships *almost all* of the time. Thus considerations of convenience, fairness, and predictability dominate the behavior of those who conduct international relations. These ordering impulses are reinforced by the logic of reciprocity (if X restricts the immunity of diplomats from Y, then Y will do the same or equivalent to X) and by the subservience of bureaucrats to rules that are in existence.[15] Even in wartime the desire to avoid chaos by the maintenance of communication and by refraining from belligerent excess gives law the important task of generating mutually acceptable norms capable of clear discernment and adequate implementation.[16] Furthermore, it is important to achieve clarity of legal rights so as to provide international life with minimum stability. Thus it is essential to have a legal mechanism for absorbing effective changes of legal status achieved on the political level by diplomacy or warfare. The peace treaty that expresses the new distribution of authority constitutes "the given" at the end of a war. This amounts to a new condition of normalcy that needs the stabilizing control of international law. Victory through force acts in the traditional system of international law as the functional equivalent to legislation and constitutional revision in domestic society. It provides a way for the community to adapt its organic law to new needs and energies that press for fulfillment.

However, the gross disadvantages and the brutalizing consequences of relying upon war to achieve changes in the prevailing order began to make statesmen seek serious alternatives in the late nineteenth century, and especially after the widespread destruction wrought by World War I. The direction of this response led to various attempts to impose rigid restrictions upon the right of a state to use international force. Most nations were persuaded to renounce the use of force in international affairs except for self-defense and to create primitive collective machinery in the League of Nations. The Geneva Protocol of 1924, although abandoned shortly after its adoption, was the first significant attempt of leading nations to prohibit recourse to aggressive war. The Treaty for the Renunciation of War (Briand-Kellogg Pact) in 1928 and the Anti-War Treaty of Rio de Janeiro in 1933 did formally commit a total of sixty-five nations to accept legal norms proscribing all nondefensive uses of force in international relations.[17]

At the same time that the idea of war was drawn into serious question, the regulation of its conduct was deeply challenged by the developing weapons technology. Submarines and aircraft made their military debut in World War I, threatening to render obsolete the entire corpus of the law of war. This was especially evident in the area of naval and air operations. Traditional notions of contraband, neutral carriage, and visit and search seemed obsolete in view of these new weapons.[18] World War II accentuated these trends,

climaxing the technological developments by the use of
atomic bombs against Hiroshima and Nagasaki, and the
legal-moral developments by the solemn trials and judgments
of Nuremberg and Tokyo that imposed criminal responsibility on many surviving leaders of Germany and Japan for
their roles in planning, preparing, and waging aggressive
war.[19] The United Nations Charter incorporates the response
of the world community in an atmosphere prior to the
emergence of the Cold War. Explicit norms oblige members
to renounce the use of force in international affairs except for
individual or collective self-defense against a prior armed attack.[20] A great part of the Charter seeks to provide a normative framework for a system of collective security in the event
that peace is endangered. It is commonplace to note that the
Cold War has transformed the Charter,[21] shifting responsibilities from the veto-paralyzed Security Council to the swelling
ranks of the General Assembly and the executive discretion of
the Secretariat. The financial crisis arising out of the controversial Congo Operation reveals limits, just as emerging political stability in the Congo suggests the achievements of the
United Nations with respect to the control of force. The future role of the United Nations is highly uncertain, depending
heavily upon whether the Soviet Union seeks to keep specific
internal wars within or without the ambit of the Cold War.
At present, the United Nations provides no direct protection
against nuclear warfare, except to provide a forum for disarmament negotiation and world community protest.[22]

   The nuclear powers seem to claim and exercise exclusive
control over their defense policies, including the privilege of
engaging in unlimited nuclear testing in the atmosphere.
Both the Soviet Union and the United States evidently base
their decisions to test upon military considerations arising
from the arms race: Neither state is publicly responsive to the

appeals for the end of all nuclear testing made by the overwhelming majority of the United Nations membership. However, United States officialdom expresses solicitude for world concern and promises maximum precautions and minimum atmospheric testing. And yet U Thant, then Acting Secretary-General of the United Nations, seemed to speak for the majority of nations when he referred to the anticipated high-altitude nuclear testing by the United States as "a manifestation of a very dangerous psychosis which is in evidence today."[23] It is not generally understood that some atmospheric testing may be essential to the stability of the system of mutual deterrence. If it appears that a first strike can paralyze the communications system of the target state, then the pressure grows severe either to pre-empt in times of expected attack or to disperse widely the authority to launch nuclear weapons. Atmospheric testing provides information about the vulnerability of communications systems that enables defense specialists to design a more stable deterrence system. The complex nature of this connection between atmospheric testing and the avoidance of nuclear war is just one of many illustrations of how difficult it is for responsible experts and officials to submit their behavior to control by world opinion or international organizations.

Here, too, a responsible decision balances the claims of the community against a national responsibility to resist totalitarian encroachment. The United States should not, however, assume that it alone desires to resist or knows best how to resist the totalitarian advance; therefore, responsible participation in an international organization such as the United Nations usually requires the subordination of national judgment to the collective will, or at least a clear public demonstration of the error or unfairness of the collective judgment.[24] We cannot discharge our moral responsibilities by insisting upon the autonomy of a national version of truth and necessity; such an insistence rejects the postulate of interdependence, as well as underplays the genuineness of the concern about nuclear weaponry felt by the supranational community. It also overlooks the resulting need to legitimate decisions about the use of international force—including nuclear testing—by an increasing reliance upon the vertical authorization.

Are nuclear weapons legitimate in warfare? This question concerns the legitimacy of the means of conducting warfare, and it is properly separate from the responsibility for initiating war.[25] If one examines the formal norms of the vertical system, it would appear that a strong case against legality exists. The analogy to poison gas, the inability to confine weapons effects to military targets,[26] the disproportionate ratio between human suffering and military advantage, the analogy to genocide and crimes against humanity are among the grounds urged to support the conclusion of illegality.[27]

The argument for the legality of nuclear weapons rests upon the justice of deterring Communist aggression and the impossibility of doing so (with sufficient reliability) by alternative means. Thus it is an argument that finds its rationale in the logic of collective self-defense and its moral justification in the responsibility of democratic societies to resist totalitarian expansion. This endorsement of legality is quite separate from discussion about the occasions that warrant recourse to nuclear weapons. Here, the argument only asserts the legitimacy of the use of nuclear weapons as a part of the right of self-defense. The duty to avoid an outbreak of nuclear war underscores the correlate need for a narrow and clear definition of self-defense once the legality of nuclear weapons is accepted.

Usually, however, the argument for legality is stated in rather formal terms that stem from the tolerance of the traditional system toward national claims that are not already the subject of an international prohibition. The classical view is that a nation can do whatever it is not explicitly forbidden from doing. This analysis can be used quite easily to support the legality of nuclear weapons. It is succinctly expressed in Article 613 of the United States Naval Instructions of 1955: "There is at present no rule of international law expressly prohibiting states from the use of nuclear weapons in warfare. In the absence of express prohibition, the use of such weapons against enemy combatants and other military objectives is permitted."[28] This claim is consistent with the traditional theory of obligation in international law, which rests upon the need for the express or implied consent of the state. Thus the United States is entitled to do whatever is not prohibited by treaty or customary norms.[29] The absence of vertical norms —that is, norms that derive from the formal (positivistic) sources of law—make decisions pertaining to the use of nuclear weapons fully a matter of national discretion.

This presents a basic theoretical problem for contemporary international law: What is the status of unilateral claims to engage in novel action for which there exists no normative experience? The same issue less dramatically underlies the United States' claim to the right to orbit espionage satellites over Soviet territory.[30] It is my contention that contemporary facts of interdependence combine with the logic of reciprocity to require a nation to do more than demonstrate the absence of a pre-existing prohibitive norm if it is to validate a controversial unilateral claim. A primary objective of rational policy for a major nation today is the maintenance of minimum international stability. However, once a unilateral claim is made, it validates, until a prohibitive norm emerges, equivalent claims by all other states. The use of atomic bombs in World War II and the initiation of nuclear tests on the high seas illustrate failures to anticipate the destabilizing effects of unilateral claims upon the future prospects for minimum order. We find that here the legal claiming process rests upon inadequate justification. For under present circumstances no claim should be asserted or validated unless it has first been found to cohere with the minimum needs of international stability.

At this stage such a demand has only theoretical relevance to the prospective use[31] of nuclear weapons,[32] for nations are devoting huge resources to the development of such weapons and their delivery systems. There appears to be every reason to expect that these nations would use nuclear weapons in "appropriate circumstances." We shift from the trivial directives of vertical norms that appear to proscribe the use of nuclear weapons in international affairs to the crucial content of horizontal norms. A horizontal norm is a descriptive proposition about what nations will probably do in light of the interplay of event, interest, conscience, and rule; it is a predictive generalization that acts as a comprehensive ground rule for behavior. Since rules of the game introduce stable limits into the system, they function in a normative capacity.[33] Therefore, an adequate description of international law must emphasize the identification of horizontal norms. This is especially true with regard to nuclear weapons, since Cold War tensions make it so difficult to achieve stability by the creation of a viable vertical regime of normative control (e.g., comprehensive disarmament).[34] Since agreement seems impossible, a lesser form of stability can be had by positing symmetrical sets of unilateral claims.[35] Such a horizontal regime has many defects when applied to the use of nuclear force. First, decisions to retaliate against violations are dangerous. Second, secrecy, threats, and bluffs prevent the communication of the actual defense policy to the potential enemy.[36]

Third, the ultimate stakes of the struggle provide an incentive to ignore normative restraints in times of heavy stress. Despite these defects, horizontal control seems to guard us somewhat against outbreak of nuclear war.[37]

There is a minimum horizontal norm: The initiating use of nuclear weapons must take place in a clear situation of individual or collective self-defense against a prior armed attack that has been carried across an international boundary and threatens the territorial integrity and political independence of an area that possesses sufficient international personality to entitle it to apply for membership as a state in the United Nations. This formulation intends to exclude colonial dependencies—for instance, Angola—from the right of nuclear self-defense by making minimum international personality a condition of use. Beyond this limiting condition, however, is one of greater generality. The use of nuclear weapons is justified only if it is indispensable to an adequate defense; preparations for defense should place maximum reliance upon non-nuclear weapons. Tactical atomic weapons should not be used except when essential to defense, and then only to restore the territory of the state that was a victim of the armed attack. Once fighting is carried on beyond the level of conventional weapons the dangers of escalation seem great, although at each level of use there should be clearly manifest an intention to make no more than a proportional response. All participation in internal wars should be strictly confined to conventional warfare. This means that nuclear weapons are "legal" only if needed as an essential part of self-defense against a sustained armed attack across a significant international boundary.[38] Furthermore, the objective of mass or strategic retaliation appears too costly under existing conditions. All actors should prepare to meet military threats by maximum reliance upon conventional weapons. If the attacking

nation is first to use nuclear weapons, then the defensive nation is entitled to make a proportionate counterstrike against
military targets.[39] An armed attack that consists of a major
nuclear attack signifies the collapse of the horizontal system.
This permits the target state to choose its own reprisal strategy, provided that suffering and destruction are not inflicted
capriciously or merely for the sake of revenge.[40] However, the
target state must not resort to nuclear weapons until there is
an actual attack. The horizontal system becomes very unstable if it provisionally authorizes preventive, anticipatory,
or pre-emptive strategies to justify an initial recourse to nuclear weapons. Restoration of the territorial *status quo* prior
to an armed attack should be the maximum legitimate lim-
ited-war objective.[41] This description of a horizontal legal
order governing the use of nuclear weapons combines observed regularities of behavior with a recommendation for
policies of self-limitation that seek to reconcile defense needs
with maximum security against the outbreak of a major nuclear war. It implies certain adjustments of military planning;
for instance, it commends the buildup of a conventional defense system in Western Europe and the Far East where there
is great danger of a violent breakdown of the present fragile
equilibria. This presentation of a sketch of a horizontal system
of legal control for nuclear weapons intends only to illustrate
a way of thinking about these problems. It is not meant as a
proposal that, in its present form, adequately responds to the
many nuances of national defense. The detailed contributions
that can be made by law and morality to international stability—including the assurance of adequate levels of national
defense—await further elaboration.

V

A Concluding Comment

The argument of this essay is that a moral policy toward the use of international force requires a simultaneous effort to increase the stability of the present international system and a readiness to defend the territorial *status quo* against armed attack. Stability is measured largely with reference to the probability of war, especially nuclear war.[1] Therefore, it is morally essential that we take all steps that decrease this probability without significantly weakening our capacity to defend the territorial *status quo*. Increased conventional armaments and restrained nuclear sharing illustrate moral responses.

It is also morally essential to take nonmilitary steps to improve the stability of the existing international system. Since violence today is largely confined to internal arenas it is important that actors in the world, especially the United Nations, seek to control domestic strife before it hardens into protracted military or paramilitary conflict. This requires an acknowledgment of the historical pressures now favorable to certain basic social transformations. For it is resistance to these transformations that leads to violent internal conflict. It becomes crucial, then, to help end "colonialism," "feudalism," and "racism" everywhere.[2] These are not "domestic" problems in an interdependent world experiencing a Cold War that could flare into a nuclear war by the interventionary responses of bloc rivals to situations of internal instability.

Moreover, it is morally essential to make a serious effort

to transform the existing international system into a safer one. This counsels the relevance of arms control and disarmament to a morally adequate force policy. We must not spare efforts to find a reliable, substitute international system that preserves the approximate territorial *status quo* without threats, crises, and the Damoclean presence of nuclear weapons. This objective transcends the fissures of the Cold War, making desirable the growth of trust and tolerance. The economic benefits of disarmament probably provide, as well, the most favorable objective conditions for the progressive liberalization of Communist societies to a point where the characterization "totalitarian" no longer fits.

International law is useful for the pursuit of each of these objectives. Its horizontal techniques of legal order help to maximize the existing international system; if horizontal norms become explicit they constitute an element of the stable environment. Horizontal legal order should generate fidelity to its basic norms, since a violation tends to intrude a destabilizing effect. Specifically, a violation heightens expectations of international violence, the avoidance of which is a unified aim of law, politics, and morality. The reality of international law depends upon the level of predictable stability achieved through the impact of reciprocal self-interest upon international behavior, rather than upon the existence of a sovereign issuing commands and backed up by an omnipotent enforcement apparatus. Thus an adequate definition of a norm of international law must extend beyond the statement of a rule to an inquiry into the procedural and institutional means available for its fulfillment in practice.

Of course, it is not enough to prohibit recourse to force, no matter how well developed the normative framework happens to be. For the controlling element is the presence or absence of social conditions that are conducive to peaceful relations. The bloody history of domestic discord expresses the limits of norms, institutions, and even policemen. Industrialized societies of democratic persuasion have reduced the incidence of internal political violence (as distinct from mere crime) by providing means for peaceful change and by seeking to overcome the crucial social injustices of the system before the victims forcibly challenge the system. Totalitarian societies achieve somewhat similar results by repressive mechanisms of terror and propaganda, together with substantial attempts to satisfy the needs of the population.

International peace depends ultimately on finding adequate means to settle serious grievances at an early stage, especially through the coercive intervention of supranational organizations. The impoverishment of so many populations suggests that enduring stability may yet hinge crucially upon a redistribution of wealth that imposes far heavier responsibilities on the richer nations to help the poorer ones. In exchange for this, effective population control will have to be practiced by national communities whose rate of population growth exceeds the rate of increase of their capacity to feed, clothe, house, and educate. Enduring peace probably depends more on this kind of double transformation than it does upon disarmament or the outcome of the Cold War.

In the meantime, however, it is imperative that we try to discourage war by the means at our disposal. At present, this imposes somewhat unacknowledged burdens on the legal order to provide norms that national actors interested in peace can accept as rules of the game. These norms are not supported by a strong sense of community obligation or by an adequate set of governmental institutions. Rather, the use of force is primarily inhibited by the fear of its self-destructive impact upon the welfare of the user. It is essential for the maintenance of peace, especially where serious conflict persists, that this perception of self-destructiveness abide. A logic of this sort seems to motivate the purer advocacies of maximum and diversified deterrence systems of national defense.

The argument made here is that a deterrent approach to the use of force is necessary but insufficient. It must be supplemented by a context of moral awareness and restraint that emphasizes the requirement that force must be used in international relations only if its net effect is likely to be beneficial. The justification of morality adds an affirmative element to the merely negative impulse of mutual deterrence to avoid self-destructive patterns of conduct. International law makes explicit the requirements of minimum morality as well as standardizes the rules of the game to guide actors with an overriding willingness to keep national behavior within safe limits. Thus the norms of the legal order mix morality with prudence and should be understood accordingly. This mixture, however, does not interfere with judgments of a particular legal norm as "good" or "bad" from a moral standpoint. There is an immanent and a judgmental role for morality in the life of the law. Brierly puts this well: ". . . too often we have been tempted to forget that the connection between law and morals is really more fundamental than their distinction, and that the ultimate basis of the obligation to obey law cannot be anything but moral."[3] To illustrate this proposition from the analysis of international force attempted here, we refer to the distinction between an unqualified prohibition of the right of a nation to initiate the use of nuclear weapons and the tolerance accorded such initiation by the horizontal norms of international law if done as a necessary part of self-defense against an armed attack. It is the conflict between morality and positive law that creates the issue of civil disobedience for all legal systems; this conflict can exist even though the particular norm of positive law is itself supported by adequate justification in view of the values that it preserves.

It is evident that an analysis of the moral and legal status of international force is an exceedingly complex matter. We rely finally upon the wisdom and conscience of individuals called upon to decide whether or not to use force in a specific instance. Abstract normative prescriptions will not help to guide behavior in a case where the resistance of totalitarian advance involves a decision to increase the risks of nuclear war. Instead, it is necessary to appraise a variety of significant variables, including a comparison of available alternative responses, before a rational decision about the use of force can be made. McDougal and Feliciano have made a major contribution by their brilliantly sustained application of a contextual appraisal to most of the major problems of the use of international force.[4] Their dominant criterion of justification is "reasonableness" in light of a balance between humane and military considerations. In addition, to a determination of reasonableness I would add a more intuitive category like "the assent of conscience" to emphasize the moral dimension of the problem. It seems to me that this additional criterion complements man's intellectual nature by an explicit reference to the relevance of his moral nature. We cannot dispense with the arbitration of conscience when we come to determine whether and when to risk or use international force. Our involvement with the variability and unreliability of conscience bears witness to the tragic contingency of our situation. However, to obscure this contingency by denying conscience is to impoverish reality.

NOTES

Chapter I

A PARTIAL FRAMEWORK FOR MORAL JUDGMENT
(pp. 3–31)

1. "Address on United States Plans for Resuming Nuclear Testing," *The New York Times*, March 3, 1962, p. 2 (text).

2. "The Prevention of World War III," 38 *Virginia Quarterly Review* 1, 3 (1962).

3. But one must avoid a facile invidiousness. Despite the achievements of governmental management of force in domestic societies, there are many more instances of civil than international war. It is simply that international war is a more pronounced threat to human security.

4. For a formulation that describes the choice as one involving value preferences rather than risk appraisals, see Robert A. Levine, "Facts and Morals in the Arms Debate," 14 *World Politics* 239–58 (1962).

5. See, e.g., criticism of the either/or approach to nuclear policy by J. C. Murray, "Theology and Modern War," in William J. Nagle (ed.), *Morality and Modern Warfare* (Baltimore: Helicon Press, 1960), pp. 69, 84.

6. Cf., for instance, Hans Kelsen, *Law and Peace in International Relations* (Cambridge, Mass.: Harvard University Press, 1942), with Julius Stone, *Quest for Survival: The Role of Law and Foreign Policy* (Cambridge, Mass.: Harvard University Press, 1961).

7. Quotations in this paragraph are taken from Carl Mayer, "Moral Issues in the Nuclear Dilemma," 22 *Christianity and Crisis* 36, 37 (March 19, 1962).

8. Ronald Steel, "Book Review," 76 *The Commonweal* No. 10, 261 (1962).

9. This point is also made in a different context by Herman Kahn

in "Some Comments on Controlled War," in Klaus Knorr and Thornton Read (eds.), *Limited Strategic War* (New York: Frederick A. Praeger, 1962).

10. There have been some recent notable efforts to combine military arguments with moral considerations. See, e.g., Thomas E. Murray, *Nuclear Policy for War and Peace* (Cleveland and New York: The World Publishing Company, 1960); Paul Ramsey, *War and the Christian Conscience* (Durham, N.C.: Duke University Press, 1961); Erich Fromm, *May Man Prevail?* (New York: Doubleday and Company, 1961); Karl Jaspers, *The Future of Mankind*, trans. E. B. Ashton (Chicago: University of Chicago Press, 1958); John C. Bennett (ed.), *Nuclear Weapons and the Conflict of Conscience* (New York: Charles Scribner's Sons, 1962); Amitai Etzioni, *The Hard Way to Peace* (New York: Collier Books, 1962); Thornton Read, *A Proposal to Neutralize Nuclear Weapons*, Policy Memorandum No. 22 (Princeton, N.J.: Center of International Studies, Princeton University, 1961). See generally the excellent compilation, "The Moral Problem of Modern Warfare: A Bibliography," by Noel Brown in Nagle (ed.), *op. cit.* (supra note 5), pp. 151–68; William Clancy (ed.), *The Moral Dilemma of Nuclear Weapons*, Essays from *Worldview, A Journal of Religion and International Affairs* (New York: The Church Peace Union, 1961); Levine, *op. cit.* (supra note 4). Also see the numerous articles appearing in *Christianity and Crisis* and *Worldview* that have been devoted to various moral problems arising from the existence of nuclear weapons.

11. Some of the philosophical problems of stating the relations between law and morality are well considered by F. S. C. Northrop, "Law, Language and Morals," 71 *Yale Law Journal* 1017 (1962).

12. Contrast this section on nuclear initiation with the description of the horizontal system of international legal order that prevails today. Cf. infra, Chapter IV, especially pp. 67–80.

13. This essay strongly rejects the claims of autonomy or self-sufficiency made on behalf of military pragmatism. Men cannot make rational uses of force in human affairs without considering the moral implications of their action, and it is not enough to invoke a vague goal like "the defeat of Communism" to justify the use of military force. True, military pragmatists often refer to their

willingness to use force as an indispensable means to preserve
other values. But their rhetoric asserts rather than demonstrates
the necessity of force. [The minimum condition of an adequate
justification of military force in current world affairs, in contrast,
requires us to examine the costs and risks that arise from the use
of a certain amount of force, as well as the costs and risks of its
nonuse. It is the balancing of these two sets of risks and costs that
provides a rational basis for a moral force policy.]

14. For an analysis of the Korean War that does suggest the
possibility of "victory" rather than "stalemate," see Raymond Aron,
On War, trans. Terence Kilimartin (New York: Doubleday and
Company, 1959), pp. 28–33.

15. Etzioni, *op. cit.* (supra note 10), p. 77 (results of a poll con-
ducted by the American Institute of Public Opinion; another poll
disclosed that 81 per cent of Americans consulted expressed a willingness to fight a war with the Soviet Union if this was needed
to hold Berlin).

16. For documentation of the assertion that American participa-
tion in the 1961 Cuban invasion was illegal, see Richard A. Falk,
"American Intervention in Cuba and the Rule of Law," 22 *Ohio
State Law Journal* 546 (1961).

17. It is important to distinguish sharply between interventionary uses of force by national and supranational actors. Had the
1961 Cuban invasion been authorized by genuine action on the
part of the Organization of American States, its legal and moral
status would change considerably. See inquiry into this issue in
Richard A. Falk, "The Legitimacy of Legislative Intervention by
the United Nations," in *Intervention,* a volume of essays scheduled
for publication by the Ohio State University Press in 1963.

18. Morton A. Kaplan, *United States Foreign Policy in a Revolutionary Age,* Policy Memorandum No. 25 (Princeton, N.J.: Center of International Studies, Princeton University, 1961), p. 43.

19. Techniques of indirect aggression can also achieve this result, but the appropriate defensive response is different. Compare
the response of self-defense to neutralize direct aggression with
the response of counterintervention to neutralize indirect aggression.

20. Article 51: "Nothing in the present Charter shall impair the
inherent right of individual or collective self-defense if an armed

attack occurs against a Member of the United Nations"; cf. also Article 2 (para. 4): "All Members shall refrain in their international relations from the threat or use of force against the territorial integrity or political independence of any state, or in any other manner inconsistent with the Purposes of the United Nations."

21. A descriptive stress upon rules should not interfere with inquiry into effectiveness. The normative quality of a rule presupposes processes for its implementation. Otherwise, the relevance of rules to life is problematic in any specific instance, for it is not the prescription that suffices, but the entire effort to regulate behavior in accordance with the prescription.

22. Besides this, a renunciation of the right to use nuclear weapons first might not be able to withstand a sustained pattern of aggressive conduct. Therefore, no leader could rely upon such a renunciation as adequate assurance that nuclear war would not result except in the event of nuclear armed attack. Setbacks in the Cold War might shift the political balance in either bloc to favor a more assertive military defense. That is, political instability in nuclear nations should serve to discourage provocative conduct despite the emergence of the moral stability that is expressed by a renunciation of the right of prior use of nuclear weapons. However, moral stability is valuable, since it guides those responsible for national defense and specifies certain limits for the pursuit of political goals as well as weakens the temptation of the other side to resort to pre-emptive strategies in times of crisis.

23. Contrast President Kennedy's reaffirmation of the defense policy adopted in 1956 that provided for possible nuclear retaliation in the event of a Soviet nonnuclear attack in Europe. There is a purposive ambiguity in this declaration. The word "possible" unaccompanied by a statement of principles that would guide decision is a central uncertainty. It evidently comprises a wish to use the threat of nuclear retaliation as a deterrent with decision-making flexibility. A further ambiguity concerns the failure to disclose whether the nuclear retaliation would be tactical (limited to the arena of combat) or strategic (extending beyond). Cf. Jack Raymond, "Strategy in War Clarified by U.S.," *The New York Times,* March 28, 1962, p. 1.

24. Note that an attack by conventional armies would also be an objective factor. As such, it would also be an appropriate occasion for military response, although—as argued in this chapter—not for a nuclear response.

25. The goal of stability is put forth often in this essay as a dominant moral and legal basis for the use of force in world affairs. Stability is correlated closely with ideas of order and equilibrium. The international system is unstable in several respects. First, it is difficult to change the *status quo* without recourse to force. This refers to the redistribution of wealth, power, and prestige *within* and *between* national communities. It also refers increasingly to similar redistribution between regions or blocs. One is familiar with the new claims asserted by the Afro-Asian nations and the Sino-Soviet bloc for an increased role in international institutions and a larger share of the world's wealth. See, e.g., B. V. A. Röling, *International Law in an Expanded World* (Amsterdam: Djambatan, 1960). Mechanisms for social change are very primitive in international relations, imposing rigidity that occasions violent responses.

Second, instability results from the absence of automatic corrective mechanisms that restore equilibrium once a breakdown of peace has taken place. Here, the notion of limiting violent conflict between nuclear powers to intranational arenas introduces a basis for an alternative form of stability—there are a series of limits in the event of breakdown rather than correcting devices. This restricts instability in Southeast Asia. Peacemaking machinery, such as the United Nations provided in the Congo, illustrates the operation of a corrective device that seeks to *restore* equilibrium rather than *limit* disequilibrium.

Third, instability exists where there are few steps between provocation and recourse to nuclear weapons in situations of tension and conflict. The tensions surrounding the future of Berlin illustrate this form of instability. Berlin has assumed the status of a symbolic issue of prestige in the Cold War rivalry, so that a solution unfavorable to either bloc would appear to be a severe defeat. The direct confrontation of military forces in Berlin, the apparent superiority of Soviet conventional force, and the rigidity of the Western commitment to defend successfully a city that is so vulnerable to conventional attack make the danger of recourse to nuclear weaponry particularly great. NATO can stabilize the defense of Berlin by improving its capacity to defend the city by conventional force.

Fourth, instability arises when some actors in the system pursue revolutionary objectives that cannot be satisfied by the existing pattern of values and relations. The international mission of Communism, if seriously pursued by powerful nations, is profoundly unstable. It also generates unstable reaction formations by nations that perceive themselves as targets of the revolutionary movement.

For an excellent application of the equilibrium theory to international affairs, see George Liska, *International Equilibrium* (Cambridge, Mass.: Harvard University Press, 1957).

26. Morton A. Kaplan and Nicholas Katzenbach, *The Political Foundations of International Law* (New York: John Wiley & Sons, 1961), p. 6.

27. The basic problem is lucidly explicated in Robert W. Tucker, *The Just War: A Study in Contemporary American Doctrine* (Baltimore: The Johns Hopkins Press, 1960), pp. 97–162.

28. There is a sharp distinction between a graduated program of unilateral initiative to induce reciprocal conduct by others and a policy of radical renunciation that is undertaken for autonomous reasons of morality and prudence. In the former case the unilateral actor seeks to find a substitute for negotiation in the struggle to end the arms race. See expositions by Charles Egerton Osgood: "Suggestions for Winning the Real War with Communism," 3 *Journal of Conflict Resolution* 131 (1959); *idem*, "A Case for Graduated Unilateral Disengagement," 16 *Bulletin of the Atomic Scientists* 127 (1960). The more radical unilateralist position seeks to option out of the arms race to reduce the prospects of nuclear war regardless of the concomitant threats to other national interests ("Better Red than dead"). Bertrand Russell, *Common Sense and Nuclear Warfare* (New York: Simon and Schuster, 1959); A. J. P. Taylor, *The Great Deterrent Myth* (1958; pamphlet).

29. For useful discussions, see Hedley Bull, *The Control of the Arms Race* (New York: Frederick A. Praeger, 1961), pp. 77–91; Etzioni, *op. cit.* (supra note 10), pp. 66–83; Erich Fromm, "The

Case for Unilateral Disarmament," in Donald G. Brennan (ed.), *Arms Control, Disarmament, and National Security* (New York: George Braziller, 1961), pp. 187–97.

30. The complicated special question of whether it is in some moral or political sense "better" for a marginal nuclear power such as Britain to adopt for itself a unilateralist position will not be considered here. The concern of this section is with the relevance of nuclear weapons to the defense of the West under current political conditions.

31. P. M. S. Blackett documents this contention that the differing nuclear strategies of the United States and the Soviet Union cause certain disarmament proposals of an apparently equivalent nature to give one side a decisive advantage. If the United States with its huge nuclear stockpile can locate Soviet delivery sites, a surprise attack can be launched with a prospect of relatively slight retaliation. The secrecy of the Soviet Union's missile sites is what gives its second strike a quality of invulnerability. This is the result that we seek to achieve by hardening our missile sites and developing a mobile strike threat. P. M. S. Blackett, "The Real Road to Disarmament," 63 *New Statesman*, March 2, 1962, pp. 295–300.

32. Even Fromm opens his presentation by saying that "There is little doubt that the proposal for a unilateral disarmament—in the broad sense of the unconditional dismantling of a country's military establishment—will be acceptable neither to the United States nor to the Soviet Union in *the immediate future*" (italics added). Fromm, in Brennan (ed.), *op. cit.* (supra note 29), p. 187.

33. For one thing, domestic power formations appear to exclude this alternative for the envisionable future. Thus advocacy is detached from the prospect of realization. This means that the advocate does not limit choice to the alternatives that are really there; it is a utopian and futile flight from reality. For a profound treatment of the link between the distribution of power and the character of moral response, see Paul J. Tillich, *Love, Power and Justice* (New York: Oxford University Press, 1954); Manfred Halpern, "The Morality of American Intervention in the Internal Affairs of Other States," Consultation No. 11 (Washington, D.C.: Council on Religion and International Affairs, 1961).

Greater attention to responsibility to world, not nat'l community. What is the best way to aid those living under the horror 94 so great it is worse than nuclear self-defense?

NOTES

34. However, the unilateral disarmament position does develop an alternative to deterrence. This permits dialogue with a sharpening of both positions in response to challenge.

35. Cf. Marshall Shulman, "Russia's Gambit on Disarmament," *The New York Times Magazine,* March 11, 1962, p. 21.

36. Hedley Bull expresses well the unrealistic quality of the claim that unilateral initiative can produce disarmament more easily than diplomacy: "It should not be imagined, however, that general nuclear disarmament is more easily brought about without international bargaining than with it: that because the powers are unable to agree on the terms of nuclear disarmament, it is easier for them not to go to the negotiating table, but to abandon their weapons separately. The purpose of multilateral disarmament negotiations is jointly to remove the anxieties that are an obstacle to unilateral disarmament." *Op. cit.* (supra note 29), p. 89.

37. It would be quite reasonable for the Soviet Union to deliver its blackmail ultimatum at a point when unilateral disarmament had proceeded far enough to confer upon the USSR a decisive military advantage in a nuclear war. Besides satisfying Soviet ambitions for world domination, such a policy would preclude a resumption of nuclear arms development as a consequence of a reversal of Western strategy and commitment. The adoption of unilateralism would not assure its continuation as a prevailing policy.

38. See the full range of inquiry in Knorr and Read (eds.), *op. cit.* (supra note 9).

39. Some exaggerate the peace-keeping potentialities of nuclear weaponry. This position in its extreme form regards nuclear weapons as a boon to mankind since the prospect of nuclear devastation is terrible enough to eliminate war and conquest as instruments of national policy. For discussion of the limits of this view, see Aron, *op. cit.* (supra note 14).

40. Cf. Albert Wohlstetter, "The Delicate Balance of Terror," 37 *Foreign Affairs* 211–34 (1959); John F. Kennedy, "Address on United States Plans for Resuming Nuclear Testing" (supra note 1).

41. Cf. Ramsey's perceptive analysis of the moral basis of a decision to conduct atmospheric tests of nuclear weapons, *op. cit.* (supra note 10), pp. 210–17.

42. See the formulations of Kenneth W. Thompson, "The Realism of Moral Purpose in Foreign Policy," 10 *Cross Currents* 201 (1960); John H. Herz, *International Politics in the Atomic Age* (New York: Columbia University Press, 1959), pp. 3–108; Kenneth N. Waltz, *Man, the State, and War* (New York: Columbia University Press, 1959).

43 Thornton Read makes this point well when he underscores the difference between conventional weapons and tactical nuclear weapons, despite the comparability of their explosive power, by saying that it is "like arguing that marijuana should not be illegal because sufficiently small amounts of it are no worse than large amounts of coffee." See Read, *op. cit.* (supra note 10), p. 19.

44. See account of the prospective use of nuclear weapons by the United States Seventh Army in Europe in *The New York Times,* June 10, 1962, sec. I, p. 1; cf. also criticism of any proposed use of threat to use tactical nuclear weapons in Europe, infra, pp. 57–58.

45. One effect of the deployment of tactical nuclear weaponry is to disperse widely the capacity to initiate nuclear war.

46. The magnitude of conventional warfare as a prelude to the nuclear potentialities of the present is well focused in Raymond Aron, *The Century of Total War*, trans. E. W. Dickes and O. S. Griffiths (New York: Doubleday and Company, 1954).

47. See Mayer, *op. cit.* (supra note 7), p. 37. In the course of Mayer's perceptive comment he adds the obvious qualification that peace sustained by nuclear deterrence is "a brittle thing, full of risks and dangers." For some depiction of the brittleness, see John Phelps and others, *Accidental War: Some Dangers in the 1960's,* Research Paper (Columbus, Ohio: Mershon National Security Program, 1960); Herman Kahn, "The Arms Race and Some of Its Hazards," in Brennan (ed.), *op. cit.* (supra note 29), pp. 89–121.

Chapter II

LAW AND MORALITY IN THE CONTEXT OF FORCE
(pp. 32–41)

1. *The Just War,* p. 3.
2. See Myres S. McDougal, "The Ethics of Applying Systems of

Authority: The Balanced Opposites of a Legal System" in Harlan Cleveland and Harold D. Lasswell (eds.), *The Ethic of Power* (New York and Evanston: Harper & Row, 1962).

3. For full depiction of this view of law, see the essays contained in Myres S. McDougal and associates, *Studies in World Public Order* (New Haven, Conn.: Yale University Press, 1960), especially chaps. I, II, XI, XII.

4. Cf. with the somewhat different emphasis of analysis in William T. Burke, "The Legal Regulation of Minor International Coercion: A Framework of Inquiry," in *Intervention* (supra, note 17 of Chapter I).

5. Something comparable, for instance, to the meditation of Thoreau; see "Civil Disobedience, 1849," in *The Portable Thoreau* (New York: The Viking Press, 1947), pp. 109–37.

6. Cf. Reinhold Niebuhr, *Moral Man and Immoral Society* (New York: Charles Scribner's Sons, 1932).

7. "Legitimacy" serves as a broad term that covers all rules and processes that produce stability in international relations. It includes the contributions of decentralized actors (e.g., the decision of a domestic court judge) and centralized actors (e.g., a General Assembly Resolution). Legitimacy arises most fruitfully from conformity to systemic behavior (see Morton A. Kaplan, *System and Process in International Politics* [New York: John Wiley & Sons, 1957]; Kaplan and Katzenbach, *The Political Foundations of International Law*) or from the reasonableness of a decision-maker in contact with relevant social, political, and legal facts (see McDougal and associates, *op. cit.* [supra note 3]).

8. Two issues should be separated: (1) The legal status of nuclear weapons (intrinsic legality or illegality, provisional legality as a reprisal or as a weapon of necessary self-defense); see Nagendra Singh, *Nuclear Weapons and International Law* (New York: Frederick A. Praeger, 1959), and Georg Schwarzenberger, *The Legality of Nuclear Weapons* (London: Stevens & Sons, 1958); (2) The general requirement that defensive force be proportional to aggressive force; see Myres S. McDougal and Florentino P. Feliciano, *Law and Minimum World Public Order* (New Haven, Conn.: Yale University Press, 1961), pp. 241–44.

9. See Hans J. Morgenthau, "The Twilight of International

Morality," 58 *Ethics* 79 (1948), where international morality is identified with an enlightened profession of national interest rather than a deceiving claim of universalism.

10. The sit-in movement illustrates a social conflict in which participants assert the precedence of the moral claim as opposed to the enactments of local law. For provocative inquiry, see Paul Ramsey, *Christian Ethics and the Sit-In* (New York: Association Press, 1961); cf. Martin Luther King, *Stride Toward Freedom* (New York: Harper and Brothers, 1958).

11. Cf. Lon L. Fuller, "Positivism and Fidelity to Law—A Reply to Professor Hart," 71 *Harvard Law Review* 630 (February, 1958). The approach to justification taken in this essay tends to deprecate the application of preformed rules to behavioral choice. It argues, instead, that a moral decision arises when we confront and balance the relative moral value of policy alternatives. In this respect it is probably correct to distinguish this view of the relation of law and morals from that of the natural-law tradition.

12. That is, force provides the capacity to coerce change; only the direction and results of change provide occasion for evaluation.

13. John Dewey, *Intelligence in the Modern World: John Dewey's Philosophy,* ed. Joseph Ratner (Modern Library Giant; New York: The Macmillan Company, 1939), p. 488.

14. Kenneth E. Boulding, "The Prevention of World War III," 8 *Virginia Quarterly Review* 1 (1962); Walter Millis *et al., A World Without War* (New York: Washington Square Press, 1961); *idem, Permanent Peace* (Santa Barbara, Calif.: Center for the Study of Democratic Institutions, 1961).

15. That is, Articles 2 (para. 3), 2 (para. 4), and 51 commit members to a renunciation of the right to use force in international relations except for purposes of individual or collective self-defense against an armed attack.

16. This has been done with imagination and vividness in McDougal and Feliciano, *op. cit.* (supra note 8), pp. 1–96.

17. Cf. Thomas C. Schelling, *The Strategy of Conflict* (Cambridge, Mass.: Harvard University Press, 1960), pp. 175–203.

18. This is developed more fully in Richard A. Falk, "American Intervention in Cuba and the Rule of Law," 22 *Ohio State Law*

Journal 546 (1961); *idem,* "Revolutionary Nations and the Quality of International Legal Order," in Morton A. Kaplan (ed.), *Revolution in World Politics* (New York: John Wiley & Sons, 1962).

19. There is a moral tension between the need for stable limits created by the firm acceptance of objective standards (e.g., no boundary-crossing) and the need to appraise particular uses of force in the light of circumstances (e.g., prior provocation short of an armed attack but deeply threatening to territorial security).

20. *The New York Times,* December 19, 1961, p. 14.

Chapter III

The International Tableau: A Double Burden of Challenge
(pp. 42–65)

1. "Some Comments on Controlled War," in Knorr and Read (eds.), *Limited Strategic War,* p. 32.

2. A similar relation of superordination and subordination is experienced in the history of federal states, especially as responsibility for the management of force tends to shift to the center. Despite such dubious notions as "interposition," asserted by the South in regard to civil rights issues, a right of self-defense is rarely claimed. In lieu of self-defense, the substate can seek ultimate recourse by claiming a right to withdraw or secede. The Federal Government, in turn, may use force to prevent this outcome as part of its right to administer events taking place within its territory.

The status of the dispute can become complicated if issues of self-determination, colonialism, and national identity are at stake; the dispute between the Congo Federal Government and secessionist Katanga is suggestive of this complexity. In general, forcible defense by the subunit in a political system disappears as soon as power is significantly centralized. Thus it is a dead issue for most domestic societies. The decentralization of power in the international system and the meager independent coercive resources of supranational actors make, in contrast, the allocation of authority between nations and supranational organizations a lively issue. The issue is presented formally often as a dispute between the claims of "domestic jurisdiction'" and those of "international concern."

It may be illuminating to ponder the federal analogy when considering how to allocate power and authority with respect to uses of force between national communities and supranational actors. This concerns both the delimitation of respective spheres of competence (that is, occasions when a nation may use force compared with the occasions when a particular international organization may use force) and the allocation of rights when force is used by an international organization against a nation.

3. In this respect we should take account of the domestic program of amelioration outlined at the Twenty-second Congress of the Communist Party of the Soviet Union in 1961. There is a relation between participation in the material benefits of a social order and control over its political processes that may result in an unintended, but effective, transformation of Soviet society into a nontotalitarian social order. See *Documents of the 22nd Congress of the CPSU*, I–III (New York: Cross Currents Press, 1961).

use to favor surrender

4. Cf. Leiba Brown and Ruth Leeds, "What the Bombs Can Do," reprinted as an appendix to Etzioni, *The Hard Way to Peace*, pp. 267–80. See also Harrison S. Brown and James Real, *Community of Fear* (Santa Barbara, Calif.: Center for the Study of Democratic Institutions, 1960).

5. Oskar Morgenstern, *The Question of National Defense* (2nd rev. ed.; New York: Random House, 1961), p. 326. See also Herman Kahn, *On Thermonuclear War* (Princeton, N.J.: Princeton University Press, 1960), p. x: "I have a firm belief that unless we have more serious and sober thought on various facets of the strategic problem than seems to be typical of most discussion today, both classified and unclassified, we are not going to reach the year 2000—and maybe not even the year 1965—without a cataclysm of some sort, and that this cataclysm will prove a lot more cataclysmic than it needs to be."

6. For an appropriate emphasis on military decision-making as a prudent choice made after an examination of feasible alternatives, see Klaus Knorr, "Limited Strategic War," in Knorr and Read (eds.), *op. cit.* (supra note 1), pp. 3–31.

7. Civil defense raises very difficult problems relating to the probability of war, the credibility of deterrence, and the solidarity of the domestic community. For an interesting opposition of viewpoints, see Herman Kahn, Erich Fromm, and Michael

Maccoby, "Debate on the Question of Civil Defense," 33 *Commentary* 1–23 (1962).

8. Cf. references given supra, note 10 of Chapter I; also Tucker, *The Just War.*

9. This applies especially within the international system, where communication between actors so often proceeds by way of threat and counterthreat; see J. David Singer, "Threat-Perception and Armament-Tension Dilemma," 2 *Journal of Conflict Resolution* 90 (1958). An explication of horizontal limits (i.e., decentralized norms self-imposed by the actors in the system) provides a weak substitute for vertical limits (i.e., centralized norms imposed upon actors in the system). International law is predominantly horizontal in character, relying for effectiveness upon self-restraint, reciprocity, and a beneficial identity of national interest and minimum world order. I have described this view of international law in some detail in "International Jurisdiction: Horizontal and Vertical Conceptions of Legal Order," 32 *Temple Law Quarterly* 295 (1959). It is difficult to provide a definition of law in a horizontal legal order. The basic horizontal norms are those essential to minimum stability given the current distribution of power in the world. The willingness of Cold War rivals to limit participation in foreign internal wars to the provision of conventional weapons is such a basic norm. An example of an intermediate horizontal norm is the act of state doctrine. Cf. Richard A. Falk, "Towards a Theory of the Participation of Domestic Courts in the International Legal Order: A Critique of Banco Nacional de Cuba v. Sabbatino," 16 *Rutgers Law Review* 1 (1961).

10. Legal positivism continues to dominate modern thinking about international law. Especially, there is a tendency to study formal rules and their elaboration into doctrine without concern for the social and institutional conditions that make for effectiveness. In part, this positivistic method reflects dissatisfaction with early writings of natural-law jurists, who identified "the law" with *de lege ferenda,* ignoring the practice of states that followed much less acceptable patterns of behavior. This was particularly true with respect to the use of force. The inability to compel conformity to the prescriptions of the naturalists made their lofty claims appear detached from the realities of international life. The

result was to make international law seem irrelevant to national behavior. Positivistic methods sought to restore the relevance of law to international relations by staking a more modest claim, namely, that a variety of transactions between states were governed by agreements and customs that were characteristically obeyed. The job of the international jurist was to collect and classify these rules into descriptive treatises. Furthermore, there was an effort to overcome the natural-law heritage by eliminating moral evaluations of particular norms. The goodness or badness of a norm was a problem for the moralist, quite outside the scientific quest of the jurist for collections and logical analyses of rules and authoritative interpretations by courts or foreign offices. This essay adopts a contrasting "ecological" approach to the study of international legal phenomena and asserts that moral criteria are an essential ecological category. Cf. Harold and Margaret Sprout, *Man-Milieu Relationship Hypotheses in the Context of International Politics* (Princeton, N.J.: Center of International Studies, Princeton University, 1956).

11. See Ramsey, *War and the Christian Conscience;* and compare John C. Ford, "The Hydrogen Bombing of Cities," and Gordon C. Zahn, "Social Science and the Theology of War," in Nagle (ed.), *Morality and Modern Warfare,* pp. 98–103, 104–25. This problem appears greater, not less, when the target state is totalitarian, for then the victims are nonparticipating captives.

12. For definitive formulations of deterrence strategy, see Glenn H. Snyder, *Deterrence and Defense* (Princeton, N.J.: Princeton University Press, 1960); Bernard Brodie, *Strategy in the Missile Age* (Princeton, N.J.: Princeton University Press, 1959); William W. Kaufmann, *The Requirements of Deterrence,* Memorandum No. 7 (Princeton, N.J.: Center of International Studies, Princeton University, 1954); Henry A. Kissinger, *Nuclear Weapons and Foreign Policy* (New York: Harper & Brothers, 1957); Arthur Lee Burns, "From Balance to Deterrence: A Theoretical Analysis," 9 *World Politics* 494 (1957).

13. On this, contrast Julius Stone, *Aggression and World Order* (Berkeley, Calif.: University of California Press, 1958), with L. B. Sohn, "The Definition of Aggression," 45 *Virginia Law Review* 697 (1959); and Quincy Wright, "The Prevention of Aggression," 50 *American Journal of International Law* 514 (1956). See the paral-

lel analysis of the scope of defensive force by Tucker, *op. cit.* (supra note 8), pp. 113–47.

14. Soviet support for a definition of aggression should not be discounted as mere opportunism or propaganda. For the legalistic approach taken toward international law pervades Soviet thinking, and it tends to emphasize rules, definitions, and doctrines. A definition of aggression may add objectivity in arenas (e.g., United Nations) where the Soviet Union has a reasonable basis to distrust the impartiality of the hostile majority. As such, negotiated definitions may encourage increased Soviet acceptance of stable outer limits for its relations with other states. It is simplistic and dangerous to discredit Soviet efforts to achieve a certain minimum international stability.

15. Transfers of power without the provision of objective standards for its application appear to make states vulnerable to the unfair whims of political majorities. The experience of the United Nations somewhat confirms this prospect. There is an increasing tendency to politicize the interpretations of Charter norms. See, e.g., "Summary Records of the Debates of the Sixth Committee [Legal] at Its Fifteenth Session in 1960."

16. A factual interdependence has always accompanied major warfare. However, the quantity and quality of dislocation have become much more severe. The novel feature of nuclear warfare and testing is that physical damage is inflicted directly upon people and food supplies of neutral and bystanding nations. Also nonparticipants are now aware that they are interdependently linked to belligerents in a way that transforms interdependence into a political force.

17. Such a fact accounts for the widespread dissatisfaction with the nation as the fundamental decision-making unit in world affairs. Paul Goodman aptly described the state as "a baroque hangover" (Goodman, Letter to the Editor, 33 *Commentary* 69 [1962]); but see the discussions of the nation in world affairs by Reinhold Niebuhr, *The Children of Light and the Children of Darkness* (New York: Charles Scribner's Sons, 1944), pp. 153–90; *idem, The Structure of Nations and Empires* (New York: Charles Scribner's Sons, 1959).

18. Cf. Gilbert C. Gidel, "Explosions nucléaires expérimentales et liberté de la haute mer," in *Foundamental* [*sic*] *Problems of*

International Law: Festschrift für Jean Spiropoulos (1957), p. 173. See also Corfu Channel Case [1949], International Court of Justice Report 4 (Judgment of April 9, 1949); *Trail Smelter* arbitration, 3 *United Nations Report of International Arbitral Awards* 1905, 1963 (1938, 1941).

19. Fritz Grob, *The Relativity of War and Peace* (New Haven, Conn.: Yale University Press, 1949), contains a complete consideration of this problem.

20. For full depiction of contemporary problems, see Julius Stone, *Legal Controls of International Conflict* (New York: Rinehart & Company, 1954); an intelligent appraisal is succinctly offered in a review of Ramsey, *War and the Christian Conscience*, by William Lee Miller, "Nuclear Morality," 6 *The Reporter*, January 18, 1962, pp. 48, 49–50.

21. It should be understood that contemporary neutralism aims primarily to achieve a posture of nonalignment in the bloc rivalry known as the Cold War and to act to prevent nuclear antagonists from using violence against one another. In contrast, traditional neutrality was concerned with remaining aloof from a war once it had commenced.

22. This principle was incorporated into the "just war" doctrine by Thomas Aquinas. See *The Summa Theological of St. Thomas Aquinas,* trans. Fathers of the English Dominican Province (1st complete American ed.; New York: Benziger Bros., 1947–48), II, Second Part of the Second Part, Question 40, pp. 1359f.

23. See full discussion of Connally Amendment (self-judging reservation attached to our acceptance of compulsory jurisdiction) in Arthur Larson, *When Nations Disagree* (Baton Rouge, La.: Louisiana State University Press, 1961), pp. 116–62.

24. Hans J. Morgenthau, "The Twilight of International Morality," 58 *Ethics* 80 (1948).

25. For a balanced depiction, see Kaplan and Katzenbach, *The Political Foundations of International Law*, pp. 83–103; John H. Herz, "Rise and Demise of the Territorial State," 9 *World Politics* 473 (1957); A. S. Miller, "Toward a Concept of National Responsibility," 5 *Yale Review* 185 (1962).

26. But the assertion of a premature universality of perspective is also self-deceiving. See Walter Schiffer, *The Legal Community of Mankind* (New York: Columbia University Press, 1954); Nei-

buhr, works cited (supra note 17). For more promising expansions of outlook on a regional level, see Ernst B. Haas, *The Uniting of Europe* (Stanford, Calif.: Stanford University Press, 1958).

27. But rational considerations may not overcome the prevalent tendency of man to engage in aggressive conduct. See Malcolm P. Sharp, "Aggression: A Study of Values and Law," 57 *Ethics* No. 4, pt. 2 (1947); Sidney Verba, "Assumptions of Rationality and Non-Rationality in Models of the International System," 14 *World Politics* 93–117 (1961).

28. "The conclusion is that expanding interdependence within a divided world arena does not necessarily undermine parochialism. On the contrary, both direct and reported contacts with contrasting ways of life enhance preoccupation with the self." Harold D. Lasswell, "Introduction: Universality Versus Parochialism," in McDougal and Feliciano, *Law and Minimum World Public Order*, p. xxv.

29. The postulate of a "bloc" to describe the Sino-Soviet alliance may become deceptive in view of the reported deepening conflicts between these two Communist monoliths. See, e.g., *The New York Times,* January 22, 1962, p. 1.

30. On this, cf. the very persuasive moral rejection of nuclear pacifism by Jaspers, *The Future of Mankind,* pp. 235–42; see also pp. 160–73.

31. It is, however, highly "immoral," in view of the costs of war, to refuse to acknowledge liberalizing tendencies within Communist societies. An acceptance of the risk of nuclear catastrophe rests upon our negative assessment of Communist ideology, societies, and objectives. We must always be eager to provide a more favorable assessment if the facts should warrant it.

32. It does not discredit the analysis of alternative strategies to achieve a preferable state of equilibrium. For instance, the provisional acceptance of the argument for deterrence does not alter the need to seek disarmament.

33. See text supra, pp. 47–49.

34. Norman Podhoretz in "The Cold War and the West: A Symposium," 29 *Partisan Review* 9, 56, 62 (1962).

35. For a persuasive outline of a conventional defense strategy for Europe, see Read, *A Proposal to Neutralize Nuclear Weapons,*

pp. 34–37. See generally Henry A. Kissinger, *The Necessity for Choice* (New York: Harper & Brothers, 1961).

36. This requires increased conventional capacities, but it also calls for great restraint with respect to nuclear sharing, decisions to use tactical atomic weapons, the Nth-country problem, and the Nth-crew problem. Dispersed control over nuclear weapons appears likely to multiply the risk of their eventual use.

37. *The New York Times,* June 10, 1962, p. 1.

38. *Ibid.*

39 *Ibid.*

40. An inflexible defense system cannot differentiate responses to varying magnitudes of threat or attack; it is, therefore, compelled to choose between self-destructive extremes of concession and catastrophe. This seems to be the fundamental moral defect of our former reliance upon a strategy of massive retaliation.

41. See supra, note 25 of Chapter I, for an attempt to designate the meaning of stability in international relations. The textual reference to stability concerns the relationship between conflict and recourse to nuclear weapons. Instability is present whenever an international actor is likely to be faced with the alternatives of political defeat and the initiation of nuclear force in the event that the existing equilibrium breaks down. As neither alternative is compatible with either national or supranational welfare, it is desirable to alter the situation so as to lessen or eliminate the risk that such a choice must be made. A prospective readjustment of the military *status quo* in Europe should not overlook this major objective. The Berlin friction point appears especially unstable, as there is the prospect both that the equilibrium currently maintained will break down at some stage and that if the breakdown is serious enough it will tempt the NATO defenders to achieve their objectives by using nuclear weapons.

42. International law cannot both bring stability to relations between nuclear powers *and* help the West in the Cold War. It is true that one could choose to use some particular norms to promote stability (e.g., diplomatic immunity) and others for Cold War strategy (e.g., the requirement that adequate compensation must accompany expropriation). Nevertheless, it remains useful to distinguish between instrumental and universal attitudes to-

ward international legal order. For important discussion see Mc-Dougal and Lasswell's "The Identification and Appraisal of Diverse Systems of Public Order," in McDougal and associates, *Studies in World Public Order*, pp. 3–41.

43. E.g., consider the contrast between legislative and popular resistance to small appropriations for foreign aid and technical assistance and the enthusiastic support of enormous military appropriations. But we should realize, as well, that the United States has given away to other nations more of its resources than a combination of all other "altruistic" nations in history.

44. Adherence to a policy of strict nonintervention by the democratic nations undoubtedly helped Hitler's totalitarian expansion. For analysis, see Richard A. Falk, "The United States and the Doctrine of Nonintervention in the Internal Affairs of Independent States," 5 *Howard Law Journal* 163, 164–74 (1959).

45. *Idem*, "American Intervention in Cuba and the Rule of Law," 22 *Ohio State Law Journal* 546 (1961).

46. See especially Samuel P. Huntington, "Patterns of Violence in World Politics," in Huntington (ed.), *Changing Patterns of Military Politics* (New York: The Free Press of Glencoe, 1962), pp. 17–50.

47. For a thoughtful repudiation of the norms supporting strict nonintervention, see Karl Loewenstein, *Political Reconstruction* (New York: The Macmillan Company, 1946).

48. The paragraphs that follow depend heavily upon the pioneer work of Myres S. McDougal, Harold Lasswell, Morton A. Kaplan, and Nicholas Katzenbach.

49. Does such adherence presuppose mutuality? The *normative* quality of noninterference does depend upon patterns of mutual adherence. However, it may still remain *prudential* to adhere to the principle if the consequence of interference is to increase significantly the risk of war.

50. It is, of course, impossible to specify the character of a symmetrical response. In fact, a nation's capabilities may not allow it to engage in symmetrical behavior. For example, if an enemy engaged in torture, would one encourage an imitative response? Or if an enemy with paramilitary superiority instigated a guerrilla war under favorable geopolitical circumstances, it would require a much costlier outlay of resources to neutralize the challenge. Sym-

metry refers to equivalence, not congruence. Thus the balancing response may involve a naval blockade or bombardment to offset the paramilitary infiltration. The violent conflicts in Southeast Asia illustrate the difficulty of defending the *status quo* by adherence to the rules of symmetry. This is partly a consequence of the unfortunate weakness of the anti-Communist elites—not a material weakness so much as a debilitating inability to satisfy the expectations of awakening and impatient domestic populations.

51. It would appear to be too destabilizing to use the United Nations to coerce minimum social changes in the societies of bloc members. In contrast, the failure to accommodate pressures for social change in non-bloc nations would also be too destabilizing. The point here is not so much to achieve worthy societies abroad as it is to guard against the instability generated by major internal wars that attract Cold War participation.

52. Would the withdrawal from the United Nations of the Union of South Africa change the role and competence of the United Nations? Note the limited grant of power claimed by the Organization over nonmembers in Article 2 (para. 6) of the Charter. This contingency has received insufficient attention from commentators to date.

53. Cf. the multilateral approach of the United States to Communist influence in Cuba at the Foreign Ministers' Conference of the OAS at Punta del Este in January, 1962, with the unilateral sponsorship of the Bay of Pigs invasion by Castro exiles in April, 1961.

54. In addition, a maximum effort should be made to provide a clear definition of an armed attack, which would be available to guide all those who must construe the legal status of provocative action.

55. In this respect, for instance, it is hard to forgive the willingness of the West to tolerate the presence of Nationalist China on the Security Council. Such a political strategy toward an emerging legal institution (the United Nations) undermines the reasonableness of reliance by any nation likely to find itself outvoted on important issues. This exploitation of legal forms is equivalent to the Soviet attempt to paralyze the United Nations with its troika proposal.

56. For some limitation on the notion of neutrality in the appli-

cation of norms of international law, see Richard A. Falk, "The Revelance of Contending Systems of Public Order to the Delimitation of Legal Competence," *Proceedings of the American Society for International Law* 173–82 (1959). Consider also the rejection of neutrality implicit in the troika principle.

57. Fidelity to normative limits (whether horizontal or vertical) is a major way that we discharge our duty to avoid nuclear war, for it honors our willingness to compromise political objectives in exchange for minimum stability.

58. This contrasts with the more popular and superficial explanation of the United States' failure—the insufficiency of force put at the disposal of the invaders. Without embarking on involved speculation, it seems desirable to observe that the success of the Cuban invasion might have opened a bigger Pandora's box than has its failure. For instance, one must not underestimate the incitement of expansive Sino-Soviet activity along the unstable periphery of the two nations or sympathetic Castroist eruptions throughout Latin America. The spirit of Castroism is not likely to be dampened by American coercion—quite the contrary.

59. We should not discount the obstacles to disarmament that arise from mere reluctance to consider it seriously. See Richard J. Barnet, *Who Wants Disarmament?* (Boston: Beacon Press, 1960).

60. Contrast Boulding, "The Prevention of World War III," and Millis, *op. cit.*, (both supra, note 14 of Chapter II), with William V. O'Brien, who regards "our future relations with communism as a life-death struggle which will end only with the defeat of one of the contestants or with the collapse of the ideological foundations of the conflict." O'Brien, "Nuclear Warfare and the Law of Nations," in Nagle (ed.), *op. cit.* (supra note 11), p. 145.

Chapter IV

INTERNATIONAL FORCE AND INTERNATIONAL LAW
(pp. 66–80)

1. *Making International Law Work* (2nd ed.; New York: Universal Distributors, 1946), p. 32.

2. "Law, Justice, and War," in James Leslie Brierly, *The Basis of Obligation in International Law and Other Papers,* eds. Sir

Hersch Lauterpacht and C. H. M. Waldock (New York: Oxford University Press, 1958), pp. 265–79, 365.

3. These distinctions somewhat revise those in Richard A. Falk, "International Jurisdiction: Horizontal and Vertical Conceptions of Legal Order," 32 *Temple Law Quarterly* 295 (1959).

4. At this stage it is rather difficult to discern whether the Communist claim of universal mission is a matter of ritual rhetoric or a serious objective. We suspect that this is an unresolved issue within the Communist world, accounting for some of the fissures in the wall. Fromm makes a provocative argument in favor of discounting Soviet global ambition. See Fromm, *May Man Prevail?*, pp. 33–138; cf. George Modelski, *The Communist International System*, Research Monograph No. 9 (Princeton, N.J.: Center of International Studies, Princeton University, 1960; See generally Cyril E. Black (ed.), *The Transformation of Russian Society: Aspects of Social Change Since 1861* (Cambridge, Mass.: Harvard University Press, 1960).

5. Cf. Werner Levi, "On the Causes of War and the Conditions of Peace," 4 *Journal of Conflict Resolution* 411 (1960).

6. See Philip C. Jessup, "Should International Law Recognize an Intermediate Status Between Peace and War?" 48 *American Journal of International Law* 98 (1954); cf. Lothar Kotzsch, *The Concept of War in Contemporary History and International Law* (Geneva: Librairie E. Droz, 1956).

7. For depiction of the efforts of international law to deal with noninterventionary uses of violences short of war—so-called forcible measures short of war—see Grob, *The Relativity of War and Peace* (supra, note 19 of Chapter III); Albert E. Hindmarsh, *Force in Peace* (Cambridge, Mass.: Harvard University Press, 1933); cf. also the Lauterpacht-Oppenheim discussions of "compulsive settlement of state differences," retorsions, reprisals, and pacific blockade in 2 *International Law* 132–49 (7th ed., 1952).

8. Alf Ross, *A Textbook of International Law*, trans. Annie I. Fausbøll (New York: Longmans, Green & Company, 1947), p. 185.

9. *Ibid.*

10. For clear expositions of the "just war" doctrine, see Kaplan and Katzenbach, *The Political Foundations of International Law*, pp. 201–10; Joachim von Elbe, "The Evolution of the Concept of

Just War in International Law," 33 *American Journal of International Law* 665 (1939).

11. See Richard R. Baxter, "The Role of Law in Modern War," 47 *Proceedings of the American Society for International Law* 90 (1953); Josef Kunz, "The Laws of War," 50 *American Journal of International Law* 313 (1956).

12. There is, of course, a fundamental objection to the permissiveness of the nineteenth-century model of deterrence. Recourse to lethal force was discouraged, if at all, by counterforce rather than by the restraining norms of law and morality. This conferred upon leaders of national units the authority to inflict death and destruction whenever it appeared advantageous to do so.

13. And even if a nation concedes the illegality of its conduct, there is no impact upon its behavior or upon the response of the international community. In such a system the legal status of a use of force is irrelevant to the attainment of order. Hence it is deceptive to accord much attention to law. In this respect the Morgenthau-Kennan view of international affairs does reorient thinking toward reality. For truly, law and morality do not deserve emphasis in a system where power is the dominant variable for the adjustment of major conflict. The critical point is that today the changes in military technology make power much less usable to resolve conflict. The capacity to devastate an enemy, with a comparable vulnerability to experience devastation, if added to the global dimension of the Cold War, makes a blatant use of force unacceptably risky. Power no longer provides sufficient security or stability even for the most powerful nations in the world. Supplemental means of achieving stability are used and needed in such an altered world. Legal institutions, norms, and procedures hence have a renewed relevance; in addition, the search for and acceptance of moral standards has autonomous validity and responds to the widely felt need for trans-political limits upon what is permissible in a world where nations arm themselves with nuclear weapons. Thus the post-World-War II patterns of world politics require us to reinterpret the relevant roles of law, morality, and power.

14. Keeton and Schwarzenberger, *op. cit.* (supra note 1), p. 32.

15. This observation is fruitfully made by Roger Fisher, "Bring-

ing Law to Bear on Governments," 74 *Harvard Law Review* 1130 (1960).

16. Kaplan and Katzenbach, *op. cit.* (supra note 10), illustrates the role of horizontal norms during the balance-of-power period of international relations.

17. For a good summary of the international movement to outlaw war, see L. B. Sohn, *Cases on United Nations Law* (Brooklyn, N.Y.: Foundation Press, 1956), pp. 845–48.

18. E.g., J. L. Kunz, "The Chaotic Status of the Laws of War and the Urgent Necessity for Their Revision," 45 *American Journal of International Law* 37 (1951).

19. For a critical evaluation, see Mr. Justice R. B. Pal, *Crimes in International Relations* (Calcutta, 1955).

20. For a good account of the control exercised by the United Nations over recourse by nations to force, see Inis L. Claude, Jr., "The United Nations and the Use of Force," *International Conciliation* No. 532, 325 (1961); cf. comment by Stanley Hoffman, "The UN and the Use of Force," 146 *New Republic,* January 9, 1962, pp. 11–13.

21. In addition to references cited in note 10, see the survey by Stanley Hoffman, "An Evaluation of the United Nations," 22 *Ohio State Law Journal* 472 (1961).

22. See Grenville Clark and L. B. Sohn, *World Peace Through World Law* (2nd rev. ed.; Cambridge, Mass.: Harvard University Press, 1958), for a comprehensive blueprint of the steps that must be taken to achieve an effective United Nations under existing world conditions. The Clark-Sohn proposals deserve serious study by students of international affairs. Their only major shortcoming results from an insufficient treatment of the political, social, psychological, and institutional problems that attend the transition from the United Nations as it is to the Clark-Sohn vision of what the organization should become. All social scientists could contribute greatly by examining in detail various aspects of the transition from one social form to another in the context of loose political affiliation such as is present in the United Nations.

23. *The New York Times,* June 6, 1962, p. 1.

24. There are difficulties here. Decisions to undertake action of dubious legal status often result from expert analysis of classified

materials. These materials bear directly upon the needs of self-defense. It is perilous to ignore or to disclose these needs, and yet to justify challenged conduct by such self-serving explanations is also inadequate. The U-2 and atmospheric testing issues suggest the dilemma.

25. A definition of aggression tries to bring law to bear upon decisions to use force, whereas the law of war concerns belligerent means and objectives for legal and illegal participants in warfare. However, the perspectives join if one allows nuclear weapons to be used *only* as a means of self-defense against an aggressor.

26. There may be certain uses of nuclear weapons that can be confined to military targets: for instance, fleet bombardments, neutron bombs.

27. Cf. Schwarzenberger, *The Legality of Nuclear Weapons*, pp. 25–54.

28. Cf. also *The Law of Land Warfare* (U.S. Army Field Manual) § 35, 18 (1956); Robert W. Tucker, *Law of War and Neutrality at Sea* (Newport, R.I.: U.S. Naval War College, 1956), pp. 54–55.

29. A classic statement of this version of the international claiming process appears in case of the S.S. "Lotus," Permanent Court of International Justice, Series A., No. 10, 19 (1927); see also Fisheries Case [1951], International Court of Justice Report 116.

30. For detailed analysis from this perspective, see Richard A. Falk, "Space Espionage and World Order: A Consideration of the Samos-Midas Program," in *Essays on Espionage*, scheduled for publication by the Ohio State University Press in 1962.

31. Justification for the use of nuclear weapons alters radically when the perspective shifts from a deterrent threat to a decision to use them. The possession of nuclear weapons may fulfill the deterrent needs of the national society, but if it fails, it is not necessarily rational or justifiable to devastate enemy populations in the course of a counterstrike. The effectiveness of the deterrent depends upon the enemy's perceiving a firmness of resolve to deliver nuclear bombs and missiles in the event of intolerable provocation. Therefore, whether or not a nation proposes to fulfill its deterrent threats, it will seek to manifest resolve in order to enhance the credibility of the threat.

32. A recent study, sensitive to moral implications, emphasizes the momentum of events that led atomic weapons on a path from scientific invention to military necessity. Robert C. Batchelder, *The Irreversible Decision, 1939–1950* (Boston: Houghton Mifflin Company, 1962).

33. Stability is itself a moral goal of high priority in the international system. Intentional or negligent conduct that reduces stability has normative significance. Therefore, the dependence of stability upon the observance of horizontal norms makes violations "illegal" and "unjustified."

34. It is important to emphasize that a vertical regime implies institutions and procedures that assure the legal rules a reasonably high expectation of compliance or enforcement in the event of noncompliance.

35. For a somewhat similar style of analysis from a nonlegal perspective, see Leo Szilard, "Are We on the Road to War?" 18 *Bulletin of the Atomic Scientists* 23–30 (April, 1962). Cf. also Bull, *The Control of the Arms Race*, p. 91, for illustrations of situations where unilateral withdrawal or initiative with respect to provocative contact points might reduce the prospect of war; also Charles E. Osgood, "Suggestions for Winning the Real War with Communism," 3 *Journal of Conflict Resolution* 131 (1959); *idem*, "A Case for Graduated Unilateral Disengagement," 16 *Bulletin of the Atomic Scientists* 127 (April, 1960); Etzioni, *The Hard Way to Peace*, pp. 60–83.

36. This creates the constant danger that a misinterpretation of a bluff will escalate into nuclear war.

37. Although it is hard to calculate the exact potential for horizontal legal order in international relations, it seems imperative that we use horizontal techniques (reciprocity, self-restraint, reasonableness, estoppel) as well as possible; this is one of the few comprehensive ways to improve the stability of a social system in which the major actors refuse to cooperate explicitly with one another.

38. E.g., it would have been illegal for an ally of Portugal to use nuclear weapons as part of an action in collective self-defense against India's armed attack upon Goa. The more difficult question is whether a nuclear power may ever use its nuclear weapons against a non-nuclear aggressor. The manpower of Communist

China makes this an important challenge to the formulation of a horizontal scheme for the legal control of nuclear force in international affairs.

39. See, however, the problem posed in note 38 when the choice is between an initiating use of nuclear weapons and a *necessary* act of self-defense.

40. Cf. Ramsey, *War and the Christian Conscience,* a comprehensive moral argument in behalf of a counterforce nuclear strategy.

41. Cf. Tucker's depiction of traditional American insistence upon the right to use defensive force to achieve unlimited objectives (e.g., unconditional surrender). *The Just War,* pp. 97–162; see also the discussion in chap. I, sec. 3, entitled "The Limit of Self-Defense."

Chapter V

A CONCLUDING COMMENT
(pp. 81–85)

1. "Stability," as distinct from a morality of international force that combines the avoidance of nuclear war with anti-totalitarianism, has only a single goal: minimum order in the international system.

2. Words like "colonialism," "feudalism," and "racism" are only shorthand identifications of clusters of related, although often quite disparate, phenomena—hence the quotation marks. The point is to discern social problems that arouse widespread concern on the supranational level and for which solutions exist that meet with the approval of the overwhelming majority of states. The choice of means appropriate to the agreed-upon end is an occasion of discord.

3. "The Basis of Obligation in International Law," in Brierly, *The Basis of Obligation in International Law and Other Papers,* p. 65; cf. this dualistic view of the relation between law and morals with typical monistic approaches that either insist with Austinian rigor upon the clarity of the distinction between what the law is and what it ought to be or with papal forthrightness deny the distinction altogether by admitting as true law only those rules that accord with what the law ought to be.

4. McDougal and Feliciano, *Law and Minimum World Public Order.*

Index

He often talks of saving new 5 from totalitarianism. As if they will have our (US) system or theirs (SU). But they will have their own. Do we oppose spread of soviet system to save selves (US) or new 5? Or both?